F-111

in action

by LOU DRENDEL

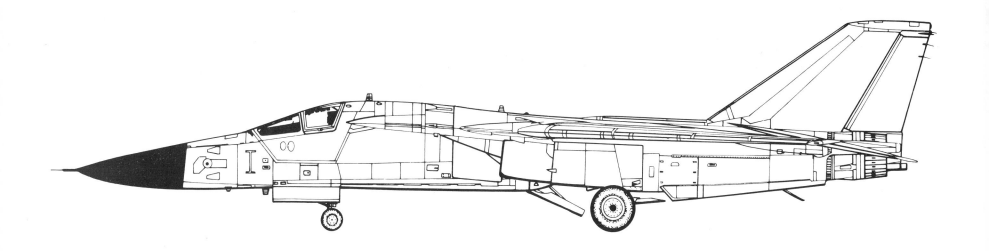

 **squadron/signal publications**

ISBN 0-89747-083-4

(Cover) Bill Wilson's F-111A penetrates the airspace over Downtown Hanoi following the course of the Red River, 22 December 1972. Moments later, having deposited his bomb load on the Hanoi docks, the swing-wing fighter was hit by ground fire. Wilson and his pilot, Bob Sponeybarger, ejected, becoming Ho Chi Minh's guests for the duration.

Photo Credits

General Dynamics
USAF
US Navy
Don Logan
Lou Drendel
Grumman
Dave Menard
Peter Mancus
Jerry Geer
Norman E. Taylor
Roger Besecker
Roger Peterson
Jim Sullivan

Introduction

So much has been written about the F-111 during it's career that it will be all but impossible to come up with anything new or startling. Ironically, the great preponderance of what has been written has been favorable, and yet most people on the fringes of the professional aviation community still regard the F-111 with the suspicion that it has been a costly mistake. There is no question about the fact that the F-111 is an expensive piece of machinery. But a mistake it is not. In fact, the Air Force has, in the F-111, exactly what it originally wanted, which is an airplane that can do all the things the F-105 could do, (which is to deliver bombs on targets deep within enemy territory by flying very fast and low enough to get under enemy radar) but with more range, accuracy, and off of airfields less than half the size required for the Thud.

The tragedy of the F-111 is that, in order to accomplish these feats, it had to pioneer in several previously untrodden technological wildernesses. This is not necessarily anything new for an advanced weapons system, but the F-111 was centerstage throughout, bathed in the harsh light of political squabbling. I guess you could say that the trouble started with the Air Force calling the F-111 a fighter, when in fact what they had asked for in Specific Operational Requirement 183, issued June 14, 1960, was a tactical strike fighter . . . really a bomber. (F-111 pilots still get testy if you call their airplane a bomber. In fact, the name tags affixed to my flight suit and flight jacket for my F-111 flight bore the inscription: "Mr. Lou Drendel, F-111 FIGHTER PILOT.") If they had called it an attack fighter, or a fighter-bomber, its mission might have been more clearly defined in the eyes of the great masses of the unwashed . . . the American Public, who were paying for it with their tax dollars. But a fighter? The name fighter carries with it the connotation of air-to-air combat, a mission never suited to the F-111. The major media, operating on the reverse of that old rule: "If you can't say something good, don't say anything." found plenty of bad things to say about the F-111, conveniently ignoring most of the good things.

If the image of what the Air Force sought in the F-111, or TFX as it was then called, was less than clear in the public mind, neither was it crystal clear in the mind of the new Secretary of Defense, Robert S. McNamara.

To further muddy the waters of the F-111 saga, enter the U.S. Navy. If you know anything at all about the American military, you may sense the ingredients for a first class political struggle with both major services involved with the acquisition of a major weapons system, which the Secretary of Defense insists must serve both . . . in completely diverse roles. McNamara, fresh from the Ford Motor Company, had decided that a billion dollars could be saved if the TFX were designed to meet USAF requirements for its strike fighter, and Navy requirements for its Fleet Air Defense Fighter. Thus was born the curse of the whole program . . . commonality. It may have been a dream worthy of the new Camelot of the Kennedy administration. But in actuality, it was a dream that was beyond the reach of technology.

From the very beginning the military was opposed to the whole concept of commonality in the TFX, and they repeatedly told McNamara so. They were basing their judgment on state-of-the-art technology, while the Secretary of Defense was determined that necessity was the mother of invention, and the commonality of the USAF/USN TFX was a definite necessity in his eyes. Unfortunately for McNamara, the modern combat aircraft is a great deal more complicated than the 1960 Ford, and in the end the initial judgment of the military proved to be all too correct.

The Navy Fleet Air Defense Fighter had been envisioned by Navy planners as a subsonic platform for the long-range Eagle missile being developed by Bendix. The Navy had contracted with Douglas to build the FADF, under the designation F-6D Missileer. If the F-6D had been built as originally planned, it would not have been anywhere near as versatile a weapons system as the Navy eventually got in its place . . . the F-14 Tomcat. But cancellation of the F-6D program was one of the last acts of President Eisenhower's Secretary of Defense, Thomas Gates, leaving the new Secretary of Defense the problem of overseeing a replacement for the Missileer. And along came Mr. McNamara with his grandiose scheme of an all-purpose airplane. In his initial proclamation on the subject, McNamara ordered that all the services (Army, Navy, Air Force, and Marines) should study development of an aircraft that could perform all of their tactical missions, including strike, close air support, air superiority, and fleet air defense. He eventually backed off on all of these requirements except the strike and fleet air defense missions, leaving the Navy and Air Force to fight for what they wanted in the resulting aircraft. If the concept of commonality was to be adhered to, a great deal of compromising was going to have to occur, and neither service wanted its mission compromised.

With the services resigned to at least going through the charade of developing the dual-service TFX, the Request for Proposals went out to industry in October 1961. Within two months, six bids from nine different companies had been received, including individual efforts by Lockheed, North American, and Boeing, and dual proposals from General Dynamics/Grumman, McDonnell/Douglas, and Republic/Chance Vought. This set the stage for further battles.

All six proposals were rejected as unsatisfactory, but the General Dynamics/Grumman and Boeing proposals seemed to be the best of what had been offered and on the strength of this, official evaluators recommended that these companies receive paid study contracts so that their offerings could be brought up to speed.

One of the healthiest raps Secretary McNamara took over the whole TFX affair was his choice of General Dynamics/Grumman to get the contract. The military had almost unanimously favored the Boeing design, (a notable exception to this was the Air Force Systems Command, which would have overall responsibility for development of the Air Force TFX) and since Vice President Johnson was from Texas, the cry of partisan politics was raised. This brought Senator McClellan's Permanent Sub-committee on Investigations into the TFX picture, and assured more muddying of the waters, as the politicians sought to manufacture political hay at the expense of the TFX.

As it turned out, the choice of General Dynamics was based on sound reasoning, and cannot be seriously faulted. In the first place, Boeing was designing their TFX around the General Electric MF-295, an engine that existed as a set of specifications only and probably could not have flown before 1967. The GD design used the Pratt & Whitney TF-30, which was to have powered the F-6D and was well along. The Boeing design also ventured into previously uncharted technological waters with the use of top-mounted engine air inlets, thrust reversers, and the use of large amounts of titanium. All of these things served to make the Boeing design look great on paper, but would have undoubtedly caused even more delays in the operational debut of the TFX. And finally, the Boeing design for the Air Force and Navy versions shared less than 50% commonality (that word again) of parts, while the GD version was 80% common in both versions. McNamara considered the Boeing proposal to be for two different airplanes. They were not playing the game according to the rules he had set forth. On November 24, 1962, he announced General Dynamics as the winner of the competition.

The award of the TFX contract did not inhibit critics within or outside of the military. Senator McClellan's committee continued to investigate the TFX contract, but in spite of several allegations of conflict of interest by members of the Department of Defense, no formal charges ever stuck. I think it is safe to say that most of these allegations were made in the interest of political advantage to those making the charges.

The Navy, on the other hand, had good reason to doubt that the General Dynamics/Grumman TFX would ever be operationally feasible. The main Navy complaint (aside from the fact that they would be getting an Air Force developed airplane) had to do with the weight of the F-111. Put very simply, it was just too heavy to operate from all but the newest and largest of Navy Carriers. In spite of a succession of programs initiated to reduce its weight, the F-111B Navy versions never got down to the required weight. The effect of these weight reducing programs, known as Weight Improvement Program, Super Weight Improvement Program, and Colossal Weight Improvement Programs I, II, and III, was to reduce the original commonality of versions from 80% to less than 30%. So, millions of dollars and seven years later, commonality was killed by Congress when it refused to fund the F-111B any further. The Navy heaved a huge sigh of relief and went on to develop the F-14. All that time and money was not wasted though, since the F-14 program did benefit from the additional development time given the remarkable Hughes AWG-9/Phoenix Missile Weapons System and the TF-30 engines.

Before describing the developmental history of the various F-111 variants, I feel it is necessary to attempt to erase some of the stigma that has dogged the F-111 since its TFX days. As I said earlier, the F-111 in service today is just about exactly what the Air Force said it wanted way back in the late 50s. If anything, it has proven to be more than the Air Force could have hoped for, since it has proven to be a remarkably adaptable platform for technological advances in avionics and engines. The only mistake made in the F-111 program of major consequence was the attempt to make it all things to all people, and refusing to accept the fact that this was technologically impossible. There have been developmental problems, but compared to all previous supersonic fighter aircraft, the F-111's safety record is amazingly good. It is with this in mind that the reader should judge whether or not the F-111 is a lemon, or one of the best combat aircraft ever produced anywhere.

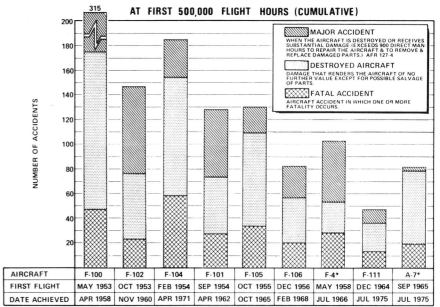

AIRCRAFT ACCIDENT COMPARISON
AT FIRST 500,000 FLIGHT HOURS (CUMULATIVE)

NUMBER OF ACCIDENTS

MAJOR ACCIDENT
WHEN THE AIRCRAFT IS DESTROYED OR RECEIVES SUBSTANTIAL DAMAGE (EXCEEDS 900 DIRECT MAN-HOURS TO REPAIR THE AIRCRAFT & TO REMOVE & REPLACE DAMAGED PARTS.) AFR 127 4

DESTROYED AIRCRAFT
DAMAGE THAT RENDERS THE AIRCRAFT OF NO FURTHER VALUE EXCEPT FOR POSSIBLE SALVAGE OF PARTS

FATAL ACCIDENT
AIRCRAFT ACCIDENT IN WHICH ONE OR MORE FATALITY OCCURS.

AIRCRAFT	F-100	F-102	F-104	F-101	F-105	F-106	F-4*	F-111	A-7*
FIRST FLIGHT	MAY 1953	OCT 1953	FEB 1954	SEP 1954	OCT 1955	DEC 1956	MAY 1958	DEC 1964	SEP 1965
DATE ACHIEVED	APR 1958	NOV 1960	APR 1971	APR 1962	OCT 1965	FEB 1968	JUL 1966	JUL 1975	JUL 1975

*INCLUDES NAVY DATA 1st 150,000 HOURS AND AIR FORCE DATA ONLY BEYOND 150,000 HOURS.

F-111 Development

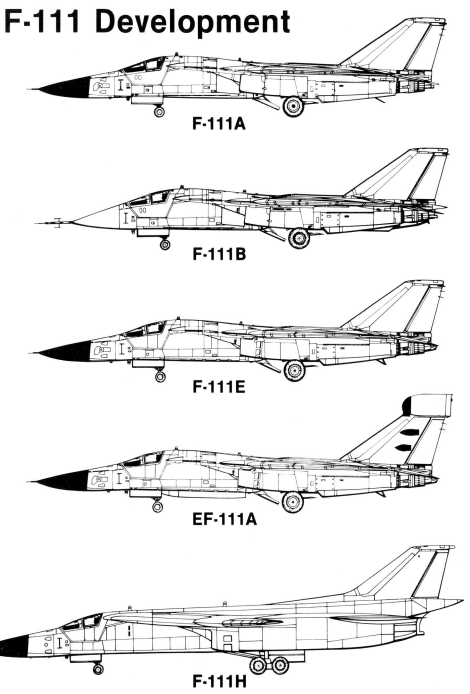

F-111A

F-111B

F-111E

EF-111A

F-111H

The first F-111A, with the main gear door, which doubles as speed brake, full out on an early test flight. The large vertical fin and rudder (112 square feet), combined with ventral fins provide high speed stability. (General Dynamics)

F-111A

This is the basic configuration. It made its first flight on December 21, 1964, sixteen days ahead of schedule. On the first flight, wings were locked at 26 degrees (maximum sweep angle at which flaps and slats can be used.) On the second flight, which was made on January 6, 1965, test pilot Dick Johnson swept the wings fully aft. This flight was made 24 days ahead of schedule and demonstration of the wing sweep mechanism at this time earned General Dynamics a bonus of $875,000. Johnson had intended to earn a further bonus by demonstrating supersonic flight at this time, but the first hint of one of the biggest headaches of the F-111 program was encountered, as the TF-30 engines demonstrated severe compressor stalls.

The TF-30 engines were the first afterburning turbofan engines, and enable the F-111 to fly long distances at medium speed with low specific fuel consumption, or to fly supersonically. The compressor stall is similar to stalling the wing of an aircraft, and is caused by excessive angle of attack or turbulent airflow. In the case of the F-111, the problem was caused by the engine inlets, but this was not immediately apparent, and the airplane was grounded while the engines went back to Pratt & Whitney for modifications. These resulted in the dash 3 variant of the TF-30 and included redesigned stator inlet and compressor spools with changed blade angles spinning at different speeds, a sixth stage bleed to increase stall tolerance at high speeds, and a new afterburner fuel control system. Even with these modifications, compressor stalls were a problem and led to the further modification of the F-111 intakes for the A model and larger intakes for subsequent models of the F-111. The TF-30 engine, marvelous technological breakthrough though it is, has caused many of the problems associated with the F-111 program, from cost escalation to crashes. (The cost of the engines tripled, while the airframe costs of the A model actually went down.) But you never saw a headline that proclaimed: "A pair of Pratt & Whitney engines crashed while attached to an F-111." General Dynamics bore the brunt of all of the bad publicity, while having little or nothing to do with government acquisition of the power plants.

5

Some of the strangest goings-on of the whole F-111 program came as a result of McNamara's personal involvement with the test program. In late 1966, the Secretary of Defense assembled the top civilian contractors in the program for weekly management meetings. General A.L. Esposito, the F-111 Project Officer in the Pentagon, was not invited to the meetings. (It was probably just as well, since the meetings themselves were somewhat of a joke, and did little more than provide ammunition for the vultures of the media.)

Meanwhile, Category I testing was continuing with the aircraft, and the F-111 was building an impressive safety record which was not shattered until the number nine aircraft was brought in to land with the wings at 50 degrees sweep, which would not have been notable had the pilot been attempting an intentional landing in that configuration. Unfortunately, he apparently thought he had the wings at 16 degrees, and landed short, destroying the aircraft.

The real disasters in the test program came in 1968. Three of six F-111s sent to Southeast Asia for combat evaluation were lost, (that episode will be covered in the Combat portion of this book) and cracks were discovered in the wing carry-through box. The F-111 was grounded while modifications were made to strengthen the assembly.

With this modification complete, it was thought that the F-111 would be able to complete the test program forthwith. Unfortunately, one of the F-111s shed a wing in December 1969 during a pull out from a low-level bomb run. Since everything had been within limits during this flight, the facts pointed to another serious flaw. The F-111 was grounded again for inspection and proof testing of every one of the 250 F-111s then in service. A flaw was found in the lower plate of the wing pivot fitting of three more of the aircraft and corrected. Though this program cost millions of dollars, it did prevent three more crashes.

By the time the test program was completed, the F-111A had the distinction of being the most thoroughly tested airplane ever flown by the USAF. (Even before it had flown it had amassed more than 20,000 hours in the wind tunnel which, compared with the F-106's 2,000 hours and the B-58's 8,300 hours, is a staggering amount.)

The test program demonstrated that the F-111 was indeed one of the best aircraft ever bought by the USAF, as every major requirement for the basic aircraft was met or exceeded. Among them: the aircraft required no more than 35 maintenance man-hours per flight hour (The first F-111 unit at Nellis AFB demonstrated a minimum of 19 and an average of 30 per aircraft), start to taxi within five minutes of alert (They did it in three minutes), required no more than 15 minutes for identifying any fault, be ready to fly 75% of the time and remain on continuous alert for five days at a time. Most encouraging of all was the enthusiastic endorsement given the F-111 by flight and ground crews at Nellis.

F-111A armament consists of conventional and nuclear weapons, including missiles and rockets. A 20mm Vulcan cannon is carried internally in the fuselage weapons bay. Weapons are also carried externally on wing pylons. The F-111A has eight wing pylons. The four inboard pylons swivel as the wings sweep so that the pylons at all times remain in line with the fuselage. The outboard pylons are used in sub-sonic flight only, and can be jettisoned if the wings are to be swept beyond 26 degrees.

The F-111A introduced some of the most sophisticated avionics ever carried on combat aircraft up to that time. These provide the capability for communications, navigation, terrain following, target acquisition and attack, penetration of enemy defenses and safe return of the airplane.

The navigation and attack set provides the crew navigation and guidance data from takeoff to landing in any weather. Used in conjunction with the aircraft's radar equipment, it provides accurate inertial navigation, course computation and automatic radar bombing capability. It constantly tells the crew the position, altitude, track and speed of the aircraft and guides it to the target by a continuous flow of commands. In addition, it supplies data for automatic radar bombing and for automatic updating of the aircraft's position. With this subsystem, the F-111 can also perform an instrument

The 12th F-111A served as test aircraft for General Dynamics, then for NASA, eventually ending up in storage at Davis Monthan AFB. (Peter Mancus via Jim Sullivan)

landing approach to any runway....even one not equipped with radio or radar landing aids.

The attack radar set performs mapping that shows a clear picture of the ground or airborne targets, regardless of visibility. It simultaneously reports the changing range between plane and target, corrects navigational errors and performs radar photography.

The terrain-following radar (TFR) can be set to fly the plane automatically at a selected low-level clearance above the ground for concealment from enemy radar. TFR guides the plane safely over the contours of the earth, day or night, dipping into valleys and skimming over mountains. The TFR constantly looks down, ahead and to each side. Signals are relayed to the autopilot for automatic flight or displayed on a cockpit instrument for manual flight. Should any of the TFR's circuits fail, the system automatically initiates a 2G pull-up. The low altitude radar altimeter constantly feeds information into the TFR on the aircraft's above-terrain altitude at any given moment.

The lead computing optical sight and missile launch computer enable the crew to fire the gun or missiles precisely by using data shown on the HUD. (Heads-Up-Display)

Early testing of weapons delivery capability, employing all eight wing pylons. The two outer pylons are fixed, but jettisonable, while the two inboard pylons remain aligned with the fuselage as the wings swing. At full gross in this configuration, the F-111A has a ceiling of less than 14,000 feet! (General Dynamics)

The fourth F-111A was the first to be fitted with the moveable wing pylons, seen here with inert Phoenix missiles. It was also fitted with a spin-recovery parachute. (USAF)

(Left) The F-111 can sweep its wings from 16 to 72.5 degrees in 24 seconds. Stability Augmentation System allows pilot to change wing position without re-trimming the aircraft. (General Dynamics)

F-111A during its first flight, December 21, 1964, with full span leading and trailing edge slats and flaps fully deployed. Slats deflect to 50 degrees inboard, 45 degrees outboard, and flaps deflect to 45 degrees. (USAF)

Fourth F-111A was left natural metal, and was used for aerodynamic testing, using tufts of thread attached to flaps. (USAF)

The seventh F-111A was fitted with extendable Sidewinder launch rails within the weapons bay. Also note cameras fitted to wing tips, under nose and mid-fuselage to record weapons launch sequences. (General Dynamics)

Sidewinder launch rails

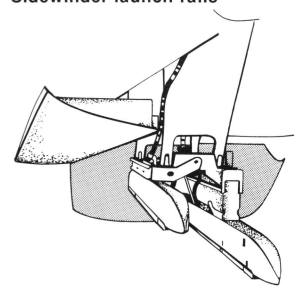

The F-111 was eventually fitted with the Vulcan 20mm cannon in weapons bay for use as the primary air-to-air weapon. (General Dynamics)

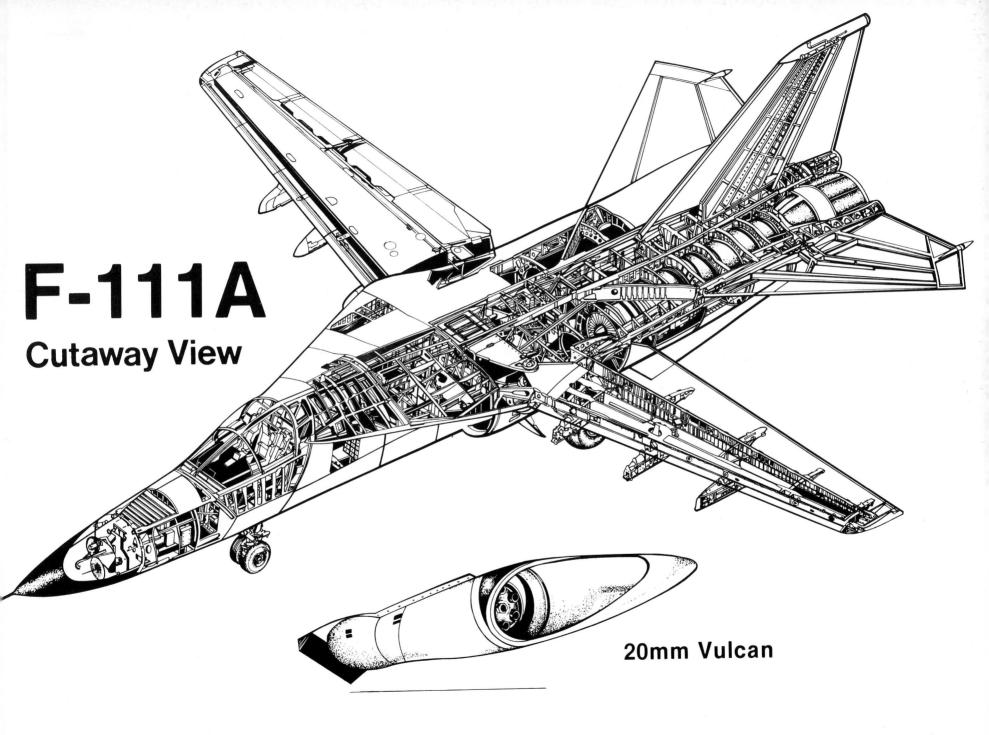

F-111A
Cutaway View

20mm Vulcan

Remarkable pair of time-lapse photos shows the incredible strength of the F-111A wing. Tests were conducted in temperature controlled chamber, and fans provided even distribution of super-cooled air over the wings. (General Dynamics)

(Above) The eighth F-111A seen during refueling tests. With wings at 26 degrees, no flap or slat extension, there is still very little elevator deflection required to maintain proper attitude on the boom. (General Dynamics)

The 10th F-111A was reconfigured for testing the proposed RF-111A. Pod under weapons bay was to have carried cameras, radar and infrared sensors, which would have been operated by computer reconnaissance control system in the cockpit. It was not funded, and no further examples were built. (General Dynamics)

Recce Pod

A "GEE WHIZ" F-111 MISSION

I might not have been salivating at the thought of flying in the F-111, but I was not in the least bit apprehensive either. As a firm believer in the non-existance of "commonality" (at least, the kind of commonality which led to the controversy surrounding the life and times of the F-111) I had tried to get as current in the operational capabilities of the long-nosed super fighter-bomber as a civilian can. After ten years of reading and clipping everything I could find on the one-eleven, I had come to the conclusion that it was probably a hell of a lot better at what it did than any other airplane in the world, and that much of the criticism it had received had been either ignorant, or self-serving, or both. I was looking forward to a first-hand demonstration of the big fighter's abilities, and by the time the big day rolled around, I was getting pretty excited about the whole thing . . . . (short of salivation).

The big day was April 5, 1976. I was scheduled to fly with an Instructor Pilot of the F-111 Fighter Weapons School at Nellis AFB, Nevada. My pilot for the flight was Captain Joe Narsavage of the 422nd Fighter Weapons Squadron, a 1966 graduate of the Air Force Academy who had spent some 2300 hours in Air Force fighters, and a third of that in the F-111. A soft-spoken six-footer, Joe Narsavage radiated quiet confidence in his own abilities, and outspoken confidence in the F-111. If there is something about the F-111 that Joe Narsavage does not know, I was not able to find out what it is in two days of talking about the airplane.

We began our preflight briefings with a session in the one-eleven simulator. The F-111 simulator, like most modern civil and military simulators, is almost as much a technological wonder as the real thing, having the capability to duplicate almost anything you can do in the airplane. There is a complete F-111 cockpit, (which is just as hard to get into as the real airplane) and behind it an L-shaped twenty foot bank of instruments, backed by computers. The panels on this six foot high array of technical wizardry are adorned with all manner of in-flight conditions, (ranging from the sublime to the terrifying) which can be shown to the crew in the simulator itself. A technician watches over all of this, and can spring any emergency on the crew that he wishes with the flick of a switch.

The F-111 can be flown by one man, but unless he has extremely long and facile arms, he is going to need some help with the right seat switchology, so we concentrated on getting me up to speed on what to turn on and when to turn it on.

Our ultimate target for the flight that afternoon was Nellis Range 62 or, as it is more popularly known, "The Dogbone". The Dogbone is a dry lake which gets its name from its shape. There is a radar reflector at one end which serves as the target. The simulator gives you a good picture of the Dogbone, and I was able to eventually put the radar cursors on the target. After an hour of playing with the radar, Joe climbed into the left seat and we went over the emergency procedures.

One of the unique features of the F-111 is its escape capsule. If the crew is forced to punch out, either crew member can initiate the ejection sequence by squeezing and pulling one of the yellow ejection handles that protrude from

Captain Joe Narsavage pre-flighting F-111A 66-018 prior to our "Gee Whiz" flight. (Lou Drendel)

the center console at his inside knee. When that happens, explosive charges separate the entire cockpit section from the rest of the airplane and a rocket motor blasts the whole thing 350 feet up, up and away from the rest of the airframe. A stabilizing drogue chute is deployed and the capsule falls to 15,000 feet before the main chute opens. Air bags are inflated under the capsule to cushion impact, and flotation balloons reminiscent of those on space capsules pop out of the top to make sure that, if you land in water, you will eventually end up right side up.

The hairiest part of a one-eleven ejection (after parachute deployment) is the landing. That is where most injuries occur, and Joe cautioned me to adjust my seat as near to a reclining position as possible. This meant getting rudder pedals all the way forward and tilting the seat back to the rear. Short guys may have the best of it in this situation, since there is room for a five-and-a-half-footer to get fairly well situated. Us six footers just have to hope for strong vertebrae.

Joe covered one emergency situation that might confront us, since we would operate in the two regimes where it is most likely to happen. It was failure of the windscreen, which might happen at mach two because of the combination of heat and dynamic pressure, or at low level as the result of a bird strike. If it did happen, he said, we could expect a lot of noise, buffeting, and junk flying around the cockpit. It would be unnerving, to say the least, and he would have his hands full, regaining and maintaining control of the airplane and, he warned me, restraining me from ejecting both of us until he was sure that the situation called for ejection. It would be impossible to talk, so everything would have to be visual. If he was incapacitated, it would be up to me to get us out. (I made damn sure I knew how to operate the ejection handle

FB-111A Simulator at Carswell AFB, Texas. Technicians at console in background can feed a wide variety of mission simulations to the crew. (General Dynamics)

by trying it out a couple of times.)

After I had been fitted with a fighter pilot's uniform, (flying suit, helmet, oxygen mask, "G" suit, gloves, and boots) we adjourned to the briefing room for a detailed look at our flight profile. Thirty-five minutes later, we were ready to go fly.

I had never seen an F-111 close up before, so when we stepped down from the line van, I was mildly surprised at its size. I mean, it's one thing to read a set of figures that tell you that the airplane can gross out at up to 50 tons, which is roughly equivalent to a whole formation of P-51s, and that it is 75 feet long, which is like three T-34s end to end, (Amazingly, the one-eleven has the same wing span as the T-34 with its wings fully swept) but it is quite another thing to walk around the bird and take it in first hand. Is that an eight foot boarding ladder? Yeah, and it doesn't even reach to the lower canopy ledge! No need to duck going under these wings . . . . the ceilings in a normal room aren't that far over my head! Sure a lot of junk hanging off the wings, though . . . . slats, flaps, rotating wing gloves . . . takes a lot of fooling of the air to get this much weight airborne, even with the wings forward. Look at the size of those tires! The damn things are better than waist-high! And those monster stabilators, whose size is accentuated by their full nose-down deflection position while the airplane is at rest . . . . there must be more square footage there than in my whole studio! The vertical fin rises more than seventeen feet in the air, and the serial number (66-018) painted on it identifies this F-111A as one of the survivors of "Combat Lancer", the first combat deployment of the F-111A, back in 1968. The paint looks like it might be eight years old too . . . . well weathered, and with the dark green undersurfaces used on Combat Lancer

aircraft. (Later camouflage schemes for TAC F-111s employ matt-black undersurfaces.) Well, enough gawking . . . . Joe is about done with the pre-flight, and it's time to climb aboard.

I climb the ladder, pausing at the top to remove helmet and mask from my helmet bag. The bag gets folded and stowed under the seat, then I climb into the cockpit. This is not like any fighter I have ever been in . . . . the seats are actually comfortable, and connecting lap belt, shoulder harness, "G" suit, and oxygen mask leads can be done easily without the aid of the solicitous crew chief, who has followed me up the ladder.

Joe is now in the left seat, and strapped in . . . . we are ready to start the engines. Somewhere behind us, and to the side, the crew chief has the APU going, and as I watch the engine instruments, the RPMs begin to build. First one, then the other mighty TF-30 lights off. The APU is disconnected and wheeled out of the way. The crew chief has stationed himself on the left side of the nose and has radio communication with us. Joe goes through the control checks, cycling the flaps and slats up and down, the wings back and forth, and the stabilators through their full travel while we wait for the Inertial Navigation System to align itself.

The INS is one of the many marvels that make the one-eleven a "Buck Rogers" airplane. it enables the one-eleven to fly anywhere in the world, without the aid of external navigational aids. All you need are the latitude and longitude of your destination, or destinations. (You can feed several separate destinations into the computer, which will dutifully store them, then direct you from one to the next.) It will also tell you exactly where you are at all times, what your true groundtrack is, and how fast you are going. Since the first part of our mission involved a mach run, we put in the end of the supersonic corridor, then the entry point for the low level run. Once into the low level portion of the mission, we would put in the additional coordinates needed to navigate our way to the target.

As the INS aligned itself, we went through some additional checks. I turned on the attack radar. (I was warned to turn it "on" only, not to "transmit", since when transmitting, it will put out high-powered beams of energy, and could injure anybody who might venture in front of our gloss black nose.) Next came closing the weapons bay doors, and checking my communications panel. Joe was busy checking the flight control and autopilot systems and the Terrain Following Radar channels. (Yet another technological miracle . . . the F-111 flight control system is self-adaptive. It senses changes in flight conditions and automatically makes adjustments for pitch, yaw, or roll deviations and gives the same control "feel" through all portions of the flight envelope, from just above stall speed to mach 2.5, and from wings full forward to full back. It is triple redundant, which means that if one circuit fails, there are two others to carry on. Only two systems of this kind have ever been installed on operational aircraft, and the X-15 had the first.)

Thirty minutes after we had arrived at the airplane, Joe leaned over and penciled our call sign onto the placard in the center of the panel, then called ground control for clearance to taxi.

"Ringo 65 cleared to taxi to runway 21. Nellis altimeter 29.86." A final salute to the ground crew, a nudge on the throttles, and we rolled onto the taxiway.

As we rolled along the taxiway, I took note of the fact that the F-111 felt like a Cadillac, especially in comparison to many other fighters, whose stiff

Captain Joe Narsavage, USAF . . . F-111 Driver par excellence. (Lou Drendel)

legs really let you feel every crack in the pavement. Midway down the taxiway, the tower called: "Ringo 65, please hold there and let that flight of F-4s out ahead of you." A Red Flag group of F-4Es, out of Seymour-Johnson AFB, is about to depart on a combat mission, and they have a schedule to meet, so we pull over and Joe demonstrates another advantage of the swing wing. Flaps and slats up, swing the wings back, and almost anybody can squeeze past!

We pulled into the last chance quick check area, where ground crews remove armament safety pins and make a final check of tires and controls before takeoff.

We are waved out of the quick check area and call for our clearance. We will be using a departure that was specifically designed for Nellis departures, and will get us into the supersonic corridor, and we are "Cleared for the block, 180 to 580" (flight levels, which indicate 18,000 to 58,000 feet).

On the runway now . . . . Joe lines up on the centerline, and advances the throttles to max afterburner. (The F-111A and E have the least powerful of the TF-30s and, with their big tires and good brakes, can do a full-power check without skidding the wheels.) I put the attack radar to "transmit", and we are off!

I had been warned not to expect outstanding acceleration, but it looks damned impressive to me! I can feel that 36,000 pounds of thrust in the seat of my pants, as the concrete rushes past that long, long nose. At 142 knots we rotate. At 157 knots we are airborne. Gear up, then the flaps are raised incrementally to maintain a 10 degree angle of attack. With the flaps full up, the slats are raised. At 300 knots the wings are swept to 26 degrees, and we head north, climbing at 350 knots, getting into position for our turn onto the supersonic track.

Normally, a high altitude mach run is only done on a functional check flight, after an aircraft has had extensive maintenance, or an engine change, and even though the possibility exists tactically that you might do a medium altitude supersonic delivery, the possibility is rare. Low altitude supersonic deliveries are much more likely. In fact, students in the F-111 Fighter Weapons School have an opportunity to make supersonic **night TFR** deliveries! Joe admits that our high altitude mach run is for the benefit of whatever "gee-whiz" value I might want to place on it. (I will admit that there is a certain pleasure in being able to say that you have been past mach 2.)

At 27,000 feet we make a 180 degree turn, heading back south to the entry point of the supersonic corridor. Joe calls Los Angeles Center, requesting permission to enter the corridor. We are cleared and he makes another 180. We are at high subsonic speed and, as he cranks in 60 degrees of bank, we get a lot of airframe buffet. The F-111 is at home when through the mach, and will perform all manner of tight turns and rolls as smoothly as glass, but at these speeds it is showing a touch of the thoroughbred's personality.

He rolls out heading north, and the twin throttles are through the detents and into max afterburner. We accelerate as we climb towards 35,000 feet. At flight level 350 we level out momentarily, then begin our quest for mach two in earnest. I am warned to hold onto anything that is not securely fastened down. Then a zero-G push over . . . . fifteen degrees nose down . . . . bits of dirt, insulation, anything that was loose on the floor is now floating past my head, to be plastered against the rear of the cockpit as we really begin to accelerate! The wings are swept all the way back to 72 degrees now, and with no "G" on the airplane, no lift is required . . . . hence no induced drag, and the arrowhead that we have become is through the mach very quickly.

In order to comply with the structure of the supersonic corridor, (it is controlled airspace, and we have to avoid other aircraft) we level off at 240, then accelerate to 640 knots CAS. We climb again when 640 knots is reached, maintaining that airspeed to 430. At 43,000, we are over the airliners passing east to west under us, and we level off again, accelerating to mach 1.85. At 1.85 we climb again . . . . this time to 50,000 feet, and the final portion of our mach run.

Level at 50,000 . . . . mach 1.85 . . . . the sky is very dark blue . . . . no sensation of speed . . . . just the mach-meter, which is not moving. We have two pylons under each wing, and the outer pylons carry Sidewinder missile launchers. They are holding us back . . . . it will take another push-over to get mach 2. Another gentle push, and we are descending. At 430 we get mach 2.01 . . . . double sonic! I take my glove off and hold the palm of my hand up to the windscreen . . . . I can feel the heat that is generated by our speed! (One of the instruments in the F-111 is a total temperature gauge that senses skin temps. If they reach their limits, a light comes on and a digital clock begins a 300 second countdown. At the end of that time, the pilot had better have begun to slow down if he doesn't want to chance structural damage. This is not the kind of problem you would expect in the A and E models, since they just won't go much over 2.25. In the newer Fs, though, with their 25,000 pound thrust engines and speeds of up to 2.5, it can be a real possibility.

Level now . . . . at 430 . . . . mach 2 plus . . . . Joe hits the intercom and says the magic words; "You want to fly it? . . . . It's your airplane." Gingerly, I take the controls . . . . "Try a roll if you want to . . . . you can use almost full deflection." That is the wrong thing to say to a T-34 pilot. My kind of roll means get the nose up first, then give it plenty of aileron, top rudder, stick forward, top rudder again, stick aft . . . . just to keep the nose on a point as you go around. We are about to gaze across the vast chasm that separates us when it comes to experience. Joe doesn't know about T-34s . . . . an aileron roll is just that . . . . he is about to find out that I don't know about rolls in high performance airplanes . . . . at mach 2, at that. OK, pull the nose just slightly, then over with the stick . . . . he said full deflection, didn't he? . . . . yeah, OK, all the way over . . . . hmmmmmm, much better roll rate than the 34 . . . . gotta stop this thing right on 360 . . . . here it comes . . . . wham! Over with the stick! . . . . Whoops! Too far! . . . . try to correct that . . . . whoops . . . . oh, hell! I have gotten us into what Joe laconically calls a "PIO" (Pilot Induced Oscillation). He takes the airplane back, and the PIO goes away, with his deft touch. We have also gotten a compressor stall on the left engine, which is not at all noticeable in the controls. He pulls the left throttle back to military power, the stall corrects itself, and it's back to full burner . . . . just that quick. He does a roll to the right, smooth as silk . . . . positive G all the way around . . . . like the horizon is moving, not the airplane. "Try it again", he says. I do another one to the left, this time I stop it right on the numbers, but again we get a compressor stall. (Later, trying to figure out why this had happened, we decided that perhaps the left engine was more susceptible to stalls caused by disturbance of the airflow at high mach numbers.) I had discovered that an aileron roll in a high performance airplane is one of the simplest of maneuvers, requiring aileron **only**, and very little of it at that. (In the F-111, the term

Full scale mock-up of the F-111 crew module. It is a self-contained, independent vehicle within the aircraft. It is pressurized and air-conditioned, and has zero-zero ejection capability. It was subjected to 4,821 wind tunnel runs, 156 parachute drops, and 276 landing tests during the test program. (Compared to 625, 73, and 20 of those tests, respectively, for the Mercury space capsule.) (General Dynamics)

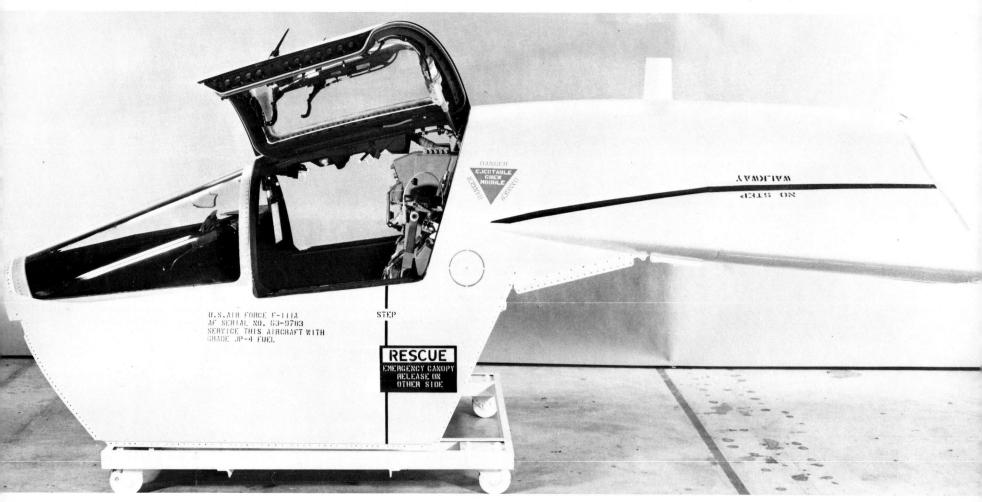

Crew Module

Crew Module Seat

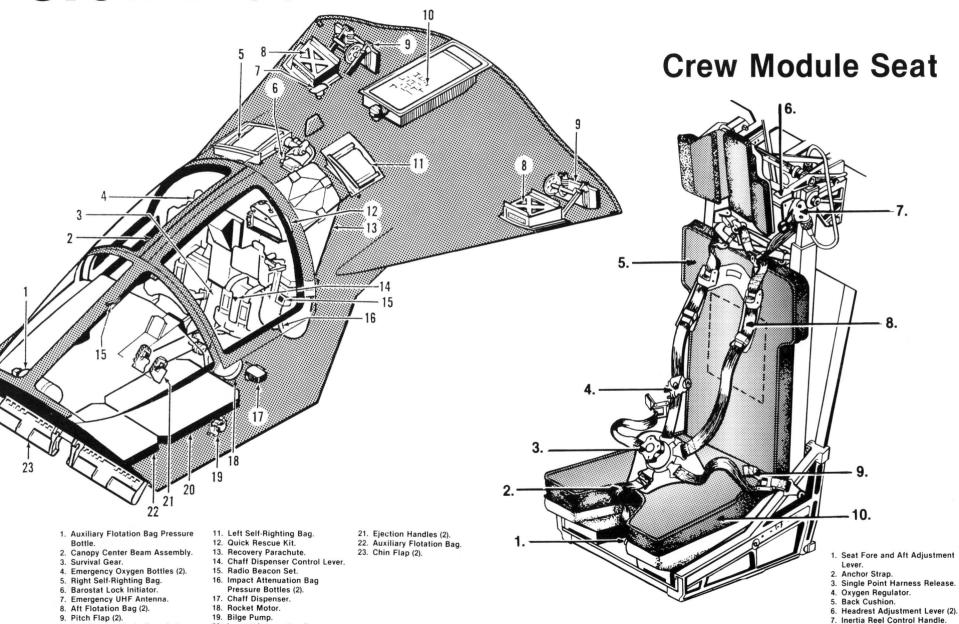

1. Auxiliary Flotation Bag Pressure Bottle.
2. Canopy Center Beam Assembly.
3. Survival Gear.
4. Emergency Oxygen Bottles (2).
5. Right Self-Righting Bag.
6. Barostat Lock Initiator.
7. Emergency UHF Antenna.
8. Aft Flotation Bag (2).
9. Pitch Flap (2).
10. Stabilization Brake Parachute.

11. Left Self-Righting Bag.
12. Quick Rescue Kit.
13. Recovery Parachute.
14. Chaff Dispenser Control Lever.
15. Radio Beacon Set.
16. Impact Attenuation Bag Pressure Bottles (2).
17. Chaff Dispenser.
18. Rocket Motor.
19. Bilge Pump.
20. Impact Attenuation Bag.

21. Ejection Handles (2).
22. Auxiliary Flotation Bag.
23. Chin Flap (2).

1. Seat Fore and Aft Adjustment Lever.
2. Anchor Strap.
3. Single Point Harness Release.
4. Oxygen Regulator.
5. Back Cushion.
6. Headrest Adjustment Lever (2).
7. Inertia Reel Control Handle.
8. Shoulder Straps (2).
9. Lap Straps (2).
10. Seat Cushion.

"aileron" is used to describe a conventional control input. The F-111 has no ailerons. At high mach numbers, roll control is through differential movement of the stabilators. At lower speeds, with the wings swept forward, spoilers on top of the wing pop out to get the roll started, then are commanded back down by the computer once the roll is established.) It is not necessary to use rudder at all for rolling maneuvers, except in the case of high angle of attack, or slow speed rolls. A person who is not very sensitive to coordinated versus uncoordinated flight would never notice the difference.

We are nearing the end of the supersonic corridor, and it is time to start our descent to the low level entry point. Normally, at this point, we would make a high G descending turn, sweeping the wings forward as we slowed down. This gets you down in the minimum time and distance. Today we have a lot of airliner traffic under us and Salt Lake City Center, whose airspace we had entered about half way through our high speed run, tells us we must extend our descent another 50 miles or so, and do it straight ahead. We have been airborne about forty-five minutes and have used 17,000 of our original 31,000 pounds of fuel. I realize how much it costs to go fast!

We are down at the low level entry point now. Normally, F-111 crews will fly either auto TFR . . . . meaning the Terrain Following Radar does all of the flying, or visual low level . . . . wherein the pilot hand-flies the airplane. The purpose of the visual low level is to enable F-111s to fly lower than the TFR if necessary to avoid enemy threats. The big catch in all this is the "visual", since F-111s mostly fly at night, or in the clag. TFR's lower limit is 200 feet . . . . when flying visually, the pilots cut that in half. Joe demonstrated both to me.

With the TFR on, and tuned, the little green scope at the upper right hand corner of the pilot's panel glows with two jagged lines. The lower line is the terrain, while the upper line represents the "command line", which tells the crew where the airplane will fly in relation to the terrain. Joe has selected "Auto TF Descent", and the airplane pushes itself over, sliding towards the barren central Nevada terrain. He has dialed in 1,000 feet on the TFR, and as smooth as silk, our thirty ton monster eases out of its dive to begin a thousand foot game of tag with the ground.

Satisfied that the TFR is performing as it should, Joe selects 200 feet, and we slide lower into the folds of rock and sagebrush. I doubt if there is a pilot alive who does not enjoy low level flight, and this must be the absolute epitome! We rush at a mountain ridge at 480 knots . . . . I glance at Joe . . . . with both of his face shields down, he is completely inscrutable, but his posture indicates a nonchalance born of absolute faith in the system. My hands itch to hover near the controls. Instead I take a picture of that onrushing pile of rocks. Then we are over it, and descending again. After the first few ridges, I am beginning to believe in the system, and enjoying the exhilaration of skimming them. Here is an opportunity to savor the breathtaking speed of the F-111. At 50,000 feet, mach 2 is impressive only because the DME looks like one of those slots in downtown Las Vegas. Down here you can really relate to your speed!

On a normal mission, the F-111 crew would try to avoid ever going over a ridge, and would spend considerable time looking at charts and figuring routes through valleys and cuts in the ridgelines before takeoff. This would involve considerable use of the INS, since it is the only navigational aid used at night or in the weather. The Whizzo (acronym for WSO . . . . Weapons System Officer) would have to be extremely adept at getting those coordinates into the

system quickly. On our mission we did a little of both: over the ridges and through the cuts. Going through the cuts was really impressive, since some of them looked barely wide enough to accomodate us. (The TFR does have a wide enough scan to assure clearance to either side. The preceding comments concerning the use of the INS apply to the F-111A. In the F-111D/F, the WSO wouldn't have to get the coordinates into the system at all. The computer memory would select them automatically, in sequence, in accordance with the preprogrammed profile. If the crew wanted to go to a point which was not on the preplanned route but was in the "destination table" he could, for example, select "D-15" (Destination 15) and the aircraft would go to it. The selection/input process would take a matter of seconds.)

If 200 feet was breathtaking, the 100 feet we were now flying at, as Joe demonstrated the hand-flown TF mission, was almost terrifying! If all pilots love low-level flight, probably most of them only love it when they are at the controls. When the machine was doing it, we were just passengers, enjoying the ride. With another pilot at the controls, you are somehow more personally involved, especially at 100 feet, and 480 knots. Joe was super-smooth, and picked his way through the rocks as no machine could have done it . . . . here was a real virtuoso performance . . . . one that I could appreciate much more than the technological marvel of TFR. You couldn't ask for a more convincing demonstration of man's mastery of his element, or of the absolute necessity to keep man as the core of any weapons system.

Blasting through a last cut in the ridgeline, we are out into a long, barren valley. The wings go back, the throttles are into afterburner, and we are through the mach at 200 feet! The ground is a blur and in my mind's eye I have a picture of the desert floor seething with clouds of dust, as the shattering impact of our supersonic shock waves race across it behind us. Again I see the face of that enemy gunner, contorted with fear and bewilderment as he tries to cope with

The author, post-flight.

F-111A of the 474th TFW, over the Nevada desert. Wing position shown is favored for high subsonic TFR missions. (General Dynamics)

this most terrifying of modern weapons delivery vehicles. If he does not see us coming, our passage will only be marked by the sense-shocking blast of our sonic boom . . . . long after we are gone.

We are on the range now, and I will try to pick out our target on the attack radar. Range 62 does not have the best radar image though, and try as I might, through a great deal of switch turning, I cannot pick it out. We are supersonic, at a couple of thousand feet, and the target comes and goes too quickly. We try again, at subsonic speeds, but it is obvious that Joe is not going to make a Whizzo out of me in one flight. Fuel considerations now force us to head for Nellis.

We climb to 18,000, call approach control, and Joe once again turns the controls over to me. I follow the ATC commands and fly the airplane to our entry point for initial. What a marvelous machine this is! The controls are so light and sensitive, yet positive . . . . it must be a very reassuring airplane to fly in IFR conditions . . . . so solid and stable . . . . gives the pilot plenty of time to get all of his other duties accomplished without worrying about wandering all over the sky.

Joe has it back now, and flies down initial at 300 knots, with the wings at 26 degrees, pitching out at mid-field. The gear comes out on downwind, followed by slats and flaps. 160 knots on base, 135 on final, and a feather touch landing. We have been airborne for an hour and fifty minutes, and I have become a thoroughly convinced proponent of the F-111.

Groundcrew loading 25 lb. practice bombs into dispenser. These practice bombs have the same ballistic properties as the 500 lb. Mk 82 low drag bomb, and allow cheap practice on the range. (USAF)

Flight of 474th TFW F-111As, with practice bomb dispensers on the inboard pylons. (Don Logan)

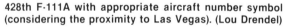

428th TFS F-111A in formation landing approach shows amount of cushion provided by main gear travel on landing. (Don Logan)

474th F-111A, with forward avionics bay open, Nellis AFB, Nevada, 1976. (USAF)

428th F-111A with appropriate aircraft number symbol (considering the proximity to Las Vegas). (Lou Drendel)

"Sweet 16", an F-111A of the 428th TFS, 474th TFW sports aircraft number and personal crew marking on nose gear door. (Lou Drendel)

Glove Vane & Door

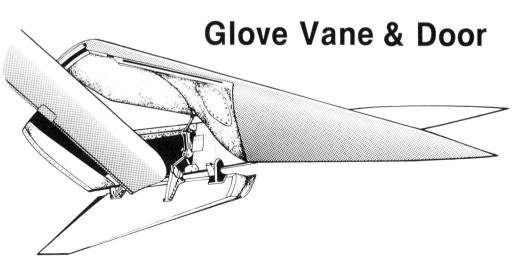

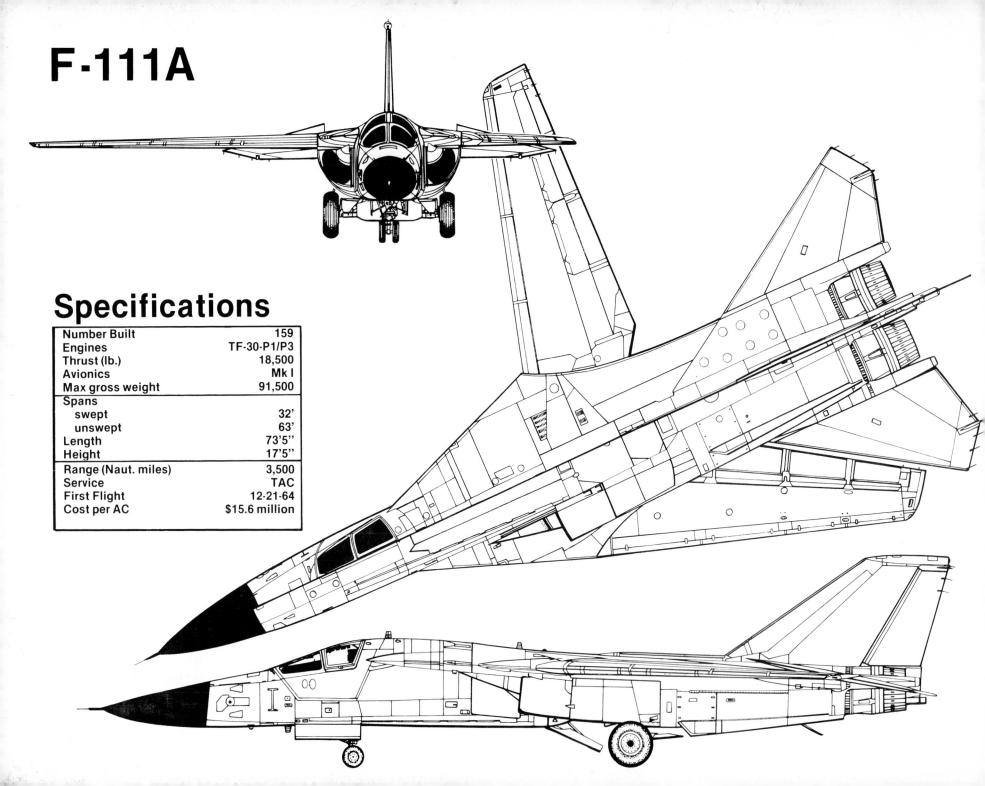

F-111A

Specifications

Number Built	159
Engines	TF-30-P1/P3
Thrust (lb.)	18,500
Avionics	Mk I
Max gross weight	91,500
Spans	
swept	32'
unswept	63'
Length	73'5''
Height	17'5''
Range (Naut. miles)	3,500
Service	TAC
First Flight	12-21-64
Cost per AC	$15.6 million

Full scale mock-up of F-111A cockpit shows location of primary flight controls and instruments. Vertical tapes on either side of attitude indicator are for airspeed and altitude readout, greatly simplifying instrument flight scan. Striped handles on either side on center console are for firing ejection system. (General Dynamics)

Crew Module Arrangement

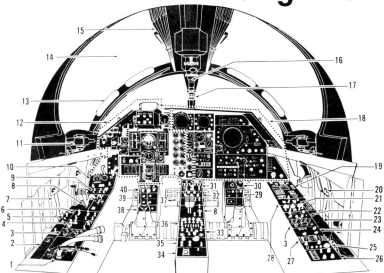

Weapons System Operator (Above) and Pilot (Below) of F-111A prepare for combat mission during 1968 Combat Lancer deployment to Southeast Asia. Crew module comfort and mobility are enhanced by the fact that the crew has the minimum of straps to wear (shoulder harness and lap belt). (USAF)

1. Left Station Oxygen-Suit Control Panel.
2. Oxygen Gage Panel.
   Electrical Power Test Panel.
3. Interphone Panel (2).
4. Auxiliary Flight Control Panel.
5. Flight Control Switch Panel.
6. Autopilot Damper Panel.
7. Left Sidewall.
8. Throttle Panel.
9. Miscellaneous Switch Panel.
10. Auxiliary Gage Panel.
11. Internal Canopy Latch Handles (2).
12. Left Main Instrument Panel.
13. Mirrors (4).
14. Canopy.

15. Thermal Curtain (2).
16. Canopy Center Beam Assembly.
17. Magnetic Compass.
18. Right Main Instrument Panel.
19. Weapons Control Panel.
    Armament Select Panel.
20. Right Sidewall.
21. Attack Radar Control Panel.
22. HF Radio Control Panel.
23. Strike Camera Control Panel.
24. ECM Control Panel.
25. CMRS Control Panel.
26. CMDS Control Panel.
27. ECM Pod Control Panel.
28. ECM Destruct Control Panel.

29. Burst Control and Target
    Elevation Panels.
30. ILS Control Panel.
31. Fuel Control Panel.
32. TFR Control Panel.
33. Electrical Control Panel.
34. Scope Camera Control Panel.
35. Air Conditioning Control Panel.
36. IFF Control Panel.
37. Ejection Handles (2).
38. Antenna Select Panel.
39. Windshield Wash/Anti-Icing
    Control Panel.
40. Compass Control Panel.

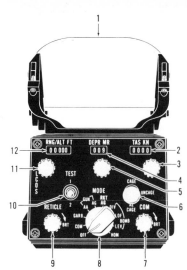

Optical Sight

1. Optical Sight.
2. Preset True Airspeed Indicator.
3. True Airspeed Set Knob.
4. Reticle Depression Indicator.
5. Reticle Depression Set Knob.
6. Aiming Reticle Cage Lever.
7. Command Bar Brightness Knob.
8. Mode Select Knob.
9. Aiming Reticle Brightness Knob.
10. Test Switch.
11. Range/Altitude Set Knob.
12. Preset Range Indicator.

General Dynamics engineers fine-tune the TF-30 in an early test aircraft. (General Dynamics)

(Below & Right) 20th TFW F-111E with forward avionics bay open, showing pull-out feature, which allows quicker and easier test and replacement of components, a feature that has cut maintenance man hours per flight hour, and endeared the F-111 to ground crews. (USAF)

Nose gear and wheel well. (USAF)

Weapons bay and door in open position. (USAF)

Landing Gear

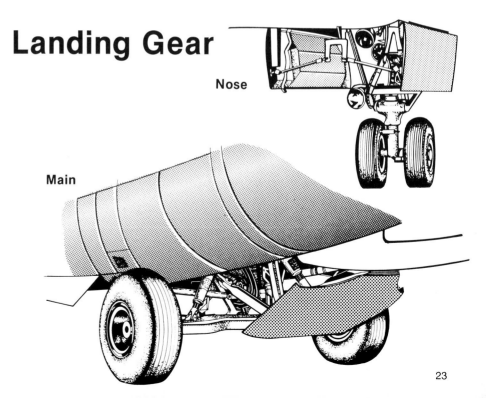

Nose

Main

Aircraft in which the author flew, seen in supersonic configuration. (General Dynamics)

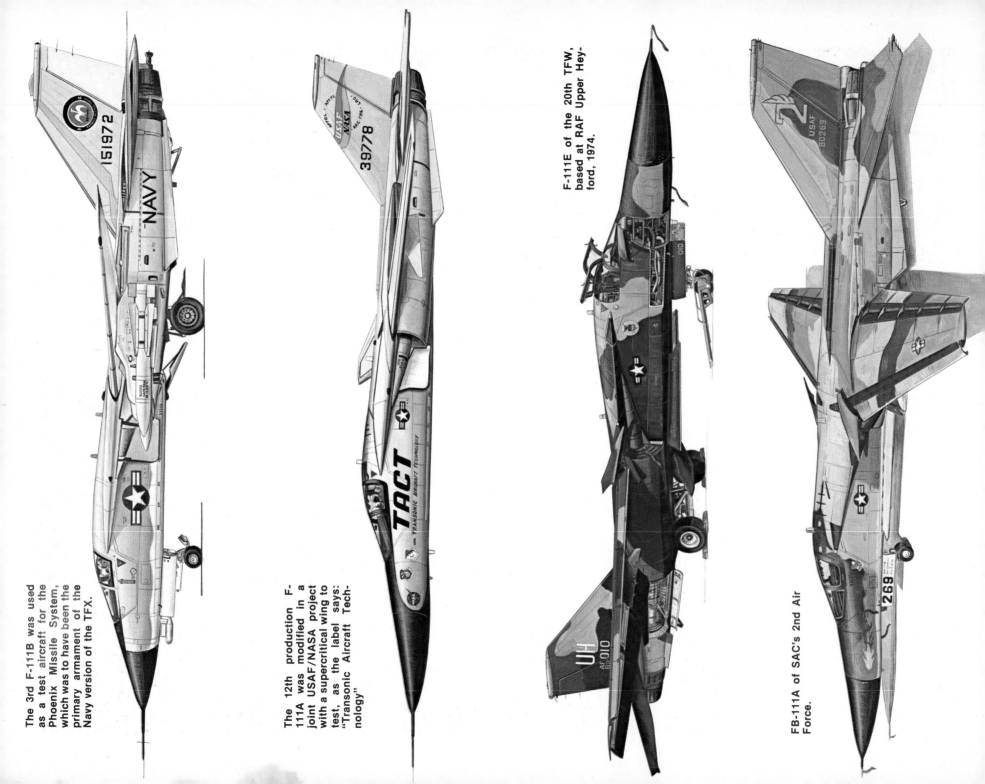

The 3rd F-111B was used as a test aircraft for the Phoenix Missile System, which was to have been the primary armament of the Navy version of the TFX.

The 12th production F-111A was modified in a joint USAF/NASA project with a supercritical wing to test, as the label says: "Transonic Aircraft Technology"

F-111E of the 20th TFW, based at RAF Upper Heyford, 1974.

FB-111A of SAC's 2nd Air Force.

(Left & Above) F-111A of 474th TFW over familiar desert terrain of southern Nevada. (Don Logan)

(Right) F-111C of the Royal Australian Air Force. (General Dynamics)

F-111 in Combat

When Bill Wilson was captured by the North Vietnamese, one of his captors pointed an accusing finger at him, exclaiming: "YOU! F-One Eleven!" and, with a sweeping palm down gesture, "WHOOOOSH!" It was a simple eloquence that described the fear and awe that the North Vietnamese felt for the swing-wing marauders that came in the night, unheralded, to sow their seeds of destruction with pin-point accuracy. When Bill collected his "Golden BB", he had been flying the F-111 for just over a year. His narrative of that year provides an in-depth look at the F-111's combat record.

"I graduated from pilot training in July 1971. After attending the mandatory survival schools, I reported to the 428th TFS, 474th TFW, at Nellis AFB, Nevada, for combat crew training in the F-111. Although I was a pilot, there was a shortage of navigators at that time, so I was assigned as a Weapons System Operator. I was still a pilot though, which meant that in addition to learning all of the black-box art associated with the F-111 right seat, I would have to maintain my flying proficiency . . . also from the right seat. By the following April, I was qualified and was flying regular missions with the wing.

When the North Vietnamese invaded South Vietnam in the Spring of 1972, we began to get preliminary alert signals. We knew that if F-111s were sent to Southeast Asia, we would be going, since ours were the only combat-ready 111s. These alert signals were secret of course, and provided some comical episodes as the entire unit stampeded the legal office to get their wills and powers of attorney up to date without telling the personnel troops what was going on. There were two false starts before we got the real order to move. After the first of these I had been assigned to the 429th TFS.

It had been decided that when we did deploy, we would try to set a record for elapsed time between the alert order and bombs-on-target. In order to do this, the two squadrons which deployed (the 429th and 430th) were divided into three groups. The first two groups were to act as ferry crews, while the third group would fly the first combat mission. The combat crews went direct to Takhli, where they had time to rest up and plan their missions. I deployed to Guam aboard a C-141, and had about 24 hours of rest before the first group arrived with the airplanes.

From Guam to Takhli was about a 6 or 7 hour flight. We hit a tanker over the Philippines, then went low level when we crossed the South Vietnamese border into Thailand. After checking the systems out, we went on in to Takhli.

The first mission was to be flown by six aircraft. We had thought that it would be a high altitude drop against the Ho Chi Minh Trail in Laos or against some of the passes leading to it in North Vietnam. This would have been a relatively safe first mission, and would have given the crews a chance to further check their systems and become acclimated to combat. Instead, the target package was changed while we were enroute to Takhli. The six crews who were to fly those missions were assigned targets in route package five, the western part of North Vietnam. (Route package 6, conceded to contain the most sophisticated and dense air defenses in the history of aerial warfare, included the Red River Delta, Hanoi, and Haiphong. Route package 5 was just to the west.)

The aircraft were on the ground about four hours for servicing, then it was night, and time to go bomb North Vietnam. Three of the six aircraft ground-aborted the mission with equipment failure, the fourth aircraft aborted in the air after his ECM equipment failed, the fifth airplane never returned from the mission, (and we never found out what happened to him) and the sixth aircraft couldn't get to his primary target and was forced to hit the alternative. Incidentally, my regular A/C, Capt. Bob Sponeybarger, flew this aircraft. It was quite a shock to get up the next morning and learn that the mission had been such a dismal failure. I'm sure more than a few people were

Using code name Combat Lancer, Detachment 1 of the 428th TFS, 464th TFW, took six F-111As to Southeast Asia in March 1968. Advertised purpose of this program was to test the F-111 in combat, but in actuality, the Air Force had hoped to temper some criticism of the F-111 program with a successful demonstration of its capabilities under real combat conditions. One of these is shown here, loaded with 6 750 lb. bombs, in its revetment at Takhli RTAB. (USAF)

remembering the premature combat trial of the 111 in 1968 and thinking: "Here we go again." (Author's note: The national news media was for sure and, though they didn't jump on the F-111 until a further three aircraft were lost, they did so with a vengeance. In their December 4, 1972, issue TIME ran a cartoon showing three F-111s in formation with lemons in place of the national insignia. They reported the following comments made by Senator William Proxmire: "The F-111 has often proved to be a death trap to its crews. The mysterious disappearance of yet another F-111 makes it appear that the Air Force is unnecessarily risking the lives of American pilots in an unsafe and defective plane." Politicians of Proxmire's ilk were a bane to the military throughout the war in Southeast Asia, often ignoring salient facts in a story in order to garner publicity for themselves. In the case of the TIME story, the facts concerning the F-111's combat record that to date were reported, but the aforementioned cartoon created an impression that was difficult to overcome, facts or no facts.)

I have my own theory about what happened to that first airplane to go down. The TFR is equipped with three modes: Hard, Medium, and Soft ride. They are graduated according to the number of G forces put on the airplane as it climbs and descends to maintain a given altitude. In gently rolling terrain, the hard ride would not produce any great discomfort. The terrain we flew through was anything but gentle. The karst is the most singular feature of North Vietnamese geography. It consists of vertical mountains, sticking straight up . . . as much as 2,000 feet straight up . . . from the rain forest and marshland. If, for example, you are at 500 feet, and your TFR sees a 2,000 foot mountain, hard ride is going to subject you to an instantaneous and constant 3Gs

Preparing 750 lb. GP bombs for loading on F-111s during Combat Lancer operation in 1968. (USAF)

until you get over that mountain, then you will be plastered against your straps with zero G as the TFR seeks that 500 foot altitude on the other side of the mountain. I know of at least one of our crews that was subjected to this, and they reported that it is an absolutely incapacitating experience. They could do nothing until the aircraft had leveled out again. When you lose command of your destiny, at night, over enemy territory, your chances for survival are noticeably depreciated. We eventually settled on the medium ride mode as the best operational setting when we had to go through the karst.

We got grounded after that mission. The systems were then checked out more thoroughly on training routes in Thailand. Our first combat missions after that were medium altitude drops on the passes just over the North Vietnamese border, in route package one.

After that we began a schedule that generally had us flying every other night. On those missions we flew alone, with no escort, and we planned our own tactics and routes to and from the targets. This gave us the best possible security, and ensured that the enemy would not be forewarned. The only people other than the crew, who would have any idea of your final run-in, would be the radar prediction people. When we had our target and had settled on the best approach to it, we would go to them for advice on the kinds of radar offsets we could expect to get for the weapons delivery system. The obvious disadvantage to this was that if you failed to return from a mission, no one had any idea of where to begin looking for you.

The consequences of these tactics . . . having little chance of being found if you went down . . . were far less important to the crews than the guaranteed factor of surprise when you hit your target. That surprise, achieved through our low level penetration, and secret ingress and egress routes, was our ticket into and out of the highest air defense threat environment ever encountered.

After the third F-111 loss, the more vocal critics of the military in general, and the F-111 in particular, began to ask questions. Of course we couldn't tell them much. Not only did we not know what had happened to the airplanes, we also did not know where it had happened. They put pressure on the military, and the upshot of the whole deal was that we were instructed to file a flight plan for each mission, showing our route to and from the target, and the times we planned to hit each turn point. We also had to call "Moonbeam", the airborne command post for operations over the north, when we hit

the turn points. We were allowed to code the calls, but they wanted to hear from us when we hit those turn points. If they didn't hear from us, they would start calling us on the radio. Now, this is a little risky, considering that you are down to within 300 feet of the ground, probably travelling at 450 knots or better, at night in the weather, and busier than hell keeping track of your navigation. You just don't have a lot of time to be calling people on the radio. Well, we never did give them the exact coordinates. They would be somewhere in that bucket alright, but to give them the exact coordinates and have that information transmitted down to Saigon . . . which we considered to be a sieve as far as security was concerned . . . Well, that just wouldn't have been healthy.

Of my 35 missions, three stand out in my mind as most memorable. On the first, we were after a rail siding on the Northeast Railway. It was snuggled deep in a valley, between 2,000 foot cliffs. The only possible way to get at it was to fly up the valley. If we had flown across the valley, our radar offsets would have been too poor to give us a chance at it. Capt. Bob Sponeybarger was my pilot on all of my missions, and we had developed our own tactics early in the campaign. Each crew had their own set of tactics, and ours were to be stabilized in the terrain following mode, at low level, before crossing the border into North Vietnam. On this mission, the weather was right down on the ground. We flew down the north side of Thud Ridge, then out around the southeast edge of it to line up with the valley. The early F-111 computers could not take much in the way of aircraft bank angle, so we had to make a very wide sweeping turn to line up. We never got above 500 feet the whole mission . . . except for one notable instance, which I will come to later. We were loaded with 12 500 pound Mark 82 "slicks", (low drag bombs) which meant we had to toss them at the target. Our standard load for the low level mission was the high drag "Snakeye" version of the Mark 82, which allowed us to stay low after release. In this case though, the valley we were in came to an abrupt end just past the target, which meant that we were going to have to pull up right after release anyway. It was very late at night, and I remember that we were concerned about getting out of route package six before daylight. The system worked like clockwork though, and we put our bombs right on the money, pulled up, and were a couple of miles off to the north before the AAA opened up. They had no idea of where we were of course, and were just firing blindly. On the way out, still in TFR, we popped over a small hill, and there on the other side was a thunderstorm. Thunderstorms held more than the normal amount of pilot fear for F-111 crews because the TFR was likely to interpret heavy concentrations of precipitation as solid terra firma, and to react accordingly. Sure enough, I didn't have time for anything more than the universally acknowledged comment for sticky situations, (Oh shit!) and we were up to 10,000 feet.

(The TFR automatically initiates a 4G pullup if it senses a "glitch" in its system, or "sees" something it would like to avoid.) Fortunately, by that time we had left the high threat area, and the only indication of enemy activity we got was an early warning radar looking at us. We got back down in the weeds though, and kept going at a high rate of knots.

Another mission that stands out in my mind occured on December 18, 1972. It was the first night of Linebacker II, and the F-111s were assigned the task of taking out all the military airfields in North Vietnam, prior to the main strike forces coming in. Our target was Hoa Lac, just southeast of Hanoi. Other aircraft were to hit Phuc Yen, Kep, Yen Bai and Bac Mai. We were in the clouds during the entire run-in to the target, but we broke out just prior to getting to the target. It was laying right in front of us, and the runways were raised just enough that they gave good radar returns. I put the crosshairs on the runway and let the computer release the bombs. Later photos showed that we got two on the taxiways and one on the runway. The airfield was shut down for the rest of Linebacker II. That whole area around Hanoi were multiple SAM rings, and I had inadvertently left one of my ECM jammers on.

My jammer began to "argue" with one of the SAM radars, which attracted its attention, and highlighted our general position. (Author's note: The exact way in which the various ECM equipment works is, of course, secret. In this case, the jammer in question was probably a deception type, designed to mask a specific target whose position was known to the anti-aircraft defenses prior to the jammer being turned on.) As soon as I turned the jammer off, they lost contact with us, as we dropped to an even lower altitude. We were clean now, with the bombs gone, and we were going like a raped ape. I believe this was the fastest I ever remember going on these missions. Our mach meter indicated .92, which I later figured to be 630 knots.

As I said before, each crew developed its own tactics. But there were several procedures that were common to all crews. One was the sweep angle on the wings during low level high speed operations. We had found that an angle between 45 and 50 degrees gave us the best trade off in speed, range, and maneuverability at low level. It was a supersonic wing, but still very efficient in other ways. I don't know of anyone who actually got supersonic in the 111 on these low-level missions, since getting through the mach at low level would require the use of afterburner, and you never wanted to use the burner at night because of the spectacular visual effect, which would have made things very easy for the AAA gunners.

The only real serious case of SAM firings at a 111 that I know of was caused by a fly-up while the crew was inbound to the target. The fly-up allowed the North Vietnamese to get them on radar, and they couldn't get low enough to lose that radar once it had them. When they got to the target, which was in the Hanoi area, it was laced with AAA fire. They plunged into it though, hit the target, and broke for home. As soon as they pulled off the target, they had a series of five SAMs fired at them. The WSO was very busy with all of his countermeasures equipment, and they managed to avoid all the anti-aircraft.

These random fly-ups gave rise to the opinion that the enemy was firing chaff rockets up into our path, in order to cause a fly-up and allow them to acquire us on their radars. Personally, I doubt this very much, since they really had no way of knowing when and where we were going to strike, and if they had, I don't see how they could have gotten the rockets to explode at a low enough altitude. And finally, the chaff, while causing a fly-up, would probably have screwed up their own radar as well.

My last mission was by far the most memorable, though the memories are anything but happy. It was our second mission of Linebacker II. Our first mission was the strike against Hoa Lac Airfield on the night of December 18. Following that mission, we had a break of four days to allow the operations people to distribute the missions equally among all of the crews. During that break, I made the mistake of asking the Ops Officer for a mission to "downtown". We had never been to any of the targets close in to Hanoi, and both Bob and I were curious about the area. We had confidence in the F-111 and our tactics, and I guess we were eager to prove that we could challenge the most formidable air defense system ever devised and survive. It

Loading 750 lb. bombs on F-111s during Combat Lancer. (USAF)

was not the first dangerous mission I had volunteered for, but I later promised myself that it was the last.

The target we were assigned was the river docks right in the center of Hanoi. Now, "downtown" was a euphemism used to describe the magic ten mile radius of the most intensive air defenses around Hanoi. I really hadn't expected to be sent right to the center of it!

We took off from Takhli about 2100, climbed to a medium altitude, and proceded up through the Plain des Jars area of Laos into the Gorilla's Head area of North Vietnam, where we began our let-down to penetration altitude.

This was December 22, which was really the height of the battle. The enemy was not as exhausted as he would become a week later, and the air defense crews were at their sharpest. We had been striking all around the Hanoi area, and, in fact, the river docks had been coming in from the south-east, since this gave the crews a more direct route out of the area, and minimized their exposure to the defenses. We figured that they would be looking more closely at these southeast approaches, so we planned our run-in to the target from the north. After stabilizing in the TFR mode, we crossed into North Vietnam at 500 feet. The closer we got to Hanoi, the more we hugged the terrain. Our last leg before turning south was on the north side of Thud Ridge, which gave us complete masking from the air defense radars. When we came around the corner and turned south, we broke out of the weather. We were at three hundred feet, and there was a broken overcast above, with a full moon showing through the breaks in the clouds. Hardly the ideal F-111 weather. Visibility under the overcast was unlimited, and we could see the lights of Hanoi in the

Typical terrain encountered in Southeast Asia, as an F-111 demonstrates TFR. Three of six F-111s in Combat Lancer were lost, the wreckage and crews of two never recovered. The wreckage of the third revealed the probable cause of the losses as being the failure of the weld joint on the rod of the control valve of the power unit of the left tailplane. Considering the fact that Category I testing has not even been completed before sending the F-111 into combat, the combat evaluation was not the disaster it was made out to be by the media. (General Dynamics)

distance. We picked up our final run-in heading at Duc Noi, about 10 miles due north of the target. At this point we were doing about 480 knots, and my impressions of the world outside the airplane are fragmentary, limited as they had to be since I was spending the majority of my time on the radar. I remember that they never did turn the lights off. They were welding the superstructure of the Paul Doumer Bridge, which we used for our radar offset in the final attack phase. We started to pick up some AAA fire, mostly 37-57mm stuff, five miles before we got to the target. It was the typical stuff, coming up in clips of five, red and orange golf balls and, though there was a lot of it, it was all behind us since they didn't have us on radar and it was all directed at our sound. At that time I remember feeling a little let-down, since I had expected much heavier resistance. We had seen bigger stuff . . . 85 and 100mm . . . on a previous mission to Thai Nguyen. We later learned that the enemy had stopped shooting the big guns at low-level high speed targets because the rapid rate of traverse required was throwing the gun crews off the gun mounts and injuring them, and they had no hope of hitting us anyway. (Author's note: Many of the civilian casualties claimed by North Vietnam to have been inflicted by U.S. bombers were actually self-inflicted by the large caliber shells detonating at low altitude and spewing shrapnel indiscriminately about the countryside.)

But, though they weren't coming close to us with their AAA, they were quite effectively tracing our path in the sky. They had developed the tactics of blasting away with small arms fire . . . straight up . . . along this path, in the hope of getting a lucky hit. Two nights previous to our mission, one of the airplanes had come back with a hit in the extreme rear of its tailpipe. The previous night an airplane had returned with a hit in the stabilator. It seemed that they were getting the hang of their new tactics. And if I had been superstitious at all, I probably wouldn't have flown the mission at all. Every one of the previous F-111s lost had a call sign ending in 3, and they had all gone down on a Monday night. December 22 was a Monday, and our call sign was Jackal 33.

Our weapons system pickled off the twelve 500 pound Snakeyes as we roared over the docks at better than 550 miles an hour. With the F-111's sophisticated system, and the good radar offset we had gotten from the Doumer Bridge, there was never much doubt that we would hit the target, and we could see the docks exploding as we rolled off the target and headed for the turn point for our initial leg back to base. As soon as we looked back in the cockpit, we saw that we had a utility hydraulic failure light. We didn't think much of it at the time . . . we hadn't felt any hits on the airplane, and we had gotten one of these lights on a previous mission. It was more of a minor irritation than anything else. But less than a minute later, we got a right engine fire warning light. We went through the bold-face procedures, shutting the engine down. (Bold face refers to the instructions for emergency operations which appear in the flight manual.) I called Moonbeam, reporting that we were off the target and had lost an engine, and they acknowledged the call.

We had just reached the first set of foothills, and I had told Bob that we could start to climb, when I heard him say: "What the hell . . . !" I looked up from the radar to see him moving the control stick like he was operating a butter churn, and I saw that the entire warning-caution light panel was lit. There was no doubt about our next move, and with Bob's command, "Eject! Eject!", we fired the capsule rockets.

Everything worked as advertised, and it was a smooth ejection. When the parachutes opened, we were in the overcast, so we didn't see the airplane hit, but we did see the glow of the explosion, and when we broke out we could see the wreckage burning fiercely. We came down on the side of a hill, and the capsule rolled over onto my side. But it was a real nice landing . . . like someone had raised your chair a couple of feet into the air and dropped it . . . and we both exited from Bob's side completely unhurt. It was probably about 2230 when we hit the ground.

Fortunately, we had attended a jungle survival school a couple of weeks previously, and the lessons learned were still fresh in our minds. We had been told to separate as soon as possible, since it is much easier for one person to hide than two. We would try to stay within a few hundred yards of each other to make the rescue as quick as possible when the Jolly Greens got to us . . . and we never doubted that they

(Above & Below) Arrival photos show the F-111 in landing configuration at touchdown. Note that spoilers are full-up (45 degrees), and that stabilators are fully deflected to dump lift and maximize braking effectiveness. (USAF)

Four years after Combat Lancer, the F-111A returned to combat in strength. First aircraft to arrive at Takhli is greeted by a contingent of high ranking officers. (USAF)

474th F-111A loaded for combat mission with 24 Mk 82 Slicks on MERs. During 1972 Southeast Asia deployment, code named Constant Guard Five, the 474th TFW flew over 4,000 combat sorties and lost six airplanes, for a loss rate of 0.15%, which is better than a lot of outfits have achieved in peacetime, but because of the mysterious nature of losses, the F-111 received a lot of bum raps. (USAF)

would come. We both had survival radios, and they were working just fine. It was the last I was to see of Bob for more than a month.

It was the beginning of the wet season in North Vietnam, and though the area we were in was not thick jungle, the tall grass was quite wet, which made for a high degree of discomfort in the cool temperature. I found what I thought was a good hiding place, and settled down to wait for daylight, and our rescuers.

The North Vietnamese were out in force by 0430 the next morning searching for us. I had picked a hiding place right next to what was apparently one of the main trails up the side of the hill, and I spent most of the day literally frozen in place. I was so motionless that I wound up with a pinched nerve in my arm, which was under me all day. Shortly after dark, the last search party of the day came up the trail and paused next to my hiding place. They had a portable radio and were listening to Radio Hanoi, which I had assumed was knocked off the air by the bombing. After what seemed like an eternity, they moved off down the mountain.

I spent the next two nights moving to new hiding places. The weather in our area was so bad that we didn't even see an airplane that we could call on our survival radios. On the third day, a flight of Sandy A-7s came into our area. Since Bob was closer to the top of the mountain, he did all the talking, relaying whatever I had to say. The clouds were still too low for them to come down through, but we were able to talk to them, and they pinpointed our position. Unfortunately, at the end of our transmission, I heard rifle fire from Bob's position.

Bob had been hiding in some vines, and the North Vietnamese had apparently heard him talking. One of them came crashing down the hill and just by chance stepped on him. The startled Vietnamese backed up, and fired. Luckily, he missed, but that brought the rest of them down on Bob. The volleys of fire I had heard were signals that they had caught an American. They trucked him off to Hanoi, and I was left alone . . . almost. The patrols in my area continued.

On the fourth day, the A-7s returned, pinpointed my position, and then said that they were low on fuel and would go out to a tanker, gas up, and return. Well, by the time they got back, the weather had socked me in and they couldn't get back down.

The next day the weather cleared, and the bombing of Hanoi resumed in earnest. I spotted a big V of A-7s outbound from their target and called them, but they wouldn't answer. Apparently they reported the call to the Sandies though, because it wasn't long before they were over me. After determining my position, they left to get a helicopter.

As luck would have it, there was just one .50 caliber gun position in the area, and the helicopter flew right over it on his approach to my position, and they really hammered him. His refueling boom was all but shot off, the co-pilot was seriously wounded, and they were leaking fuel. To his credit, the pilot still tried for the pick-up. I

had not given them real explicit instructions on my position though, and they came to a hover about twenty feet from me, on the steep side of the hill. I decided that it was now or never, and made a run for the penetrator, which was on the end of the cable. Just as I was about to make a grab for it, I lost my footing and the downwash from the big HH-53 knocked me to the ground. I did a backflip, and rolled down the hill. When I got up, the helicopter was leaving. I can't really blame them . . . they were pretty well shot up, and may have thought that I had been hit by ground fire. As it was, they just barely made it out to a Lima Site in Laos, where the back-up Jolly Green picked them up. I later learned from the Combat Cameraman on that helicopter that the North Vietnamese were running towards them, firing their AK-47s, while they hovered over me.

Why the North Vietnamese didn't really comb the area I'll never know . . . they must have known the helicopter was trying to get someone. But they didn't, and I moved again that night.

By this time, the two pints of water that had been in my survival gear was long since gone, and I was getting mighty thirsty. The light misty rain that fell most of the time only served to keep me wet, cold and miserable. The jungle instructors had told us about the water vines and bamboo that existed in North Vietnam, but they had neglected to tell us that they were dry until well into the wet season. I drilled into several of these looking for water, but only found cool air. While I was hiding the next day, several Vietnamese came up the trail close to where I was. I would swear that one of them spotted one of those drilled bamboo, and exclaimed: "LOOK! AMERICAN!" Anyway, whatever he said precipitated a search of the area. I heard one of them coming my way, and tucked everything in. I had lost my mosquito net in the jump for the helicopter, and that had provided most of the camouflage for my face. I put my gloved hand over my face, and held my breath. I heard and felt the grass being parted over my head, but again my luck held and he didn't see me.

Shortly after that, a flight of F-4s came into the area and called me on the radio. The flight lead spotted my position and told me to move to a better area for pick-up. Rather than give instructions that the North Vietnamese might overhear and understand, he told me to move from Nellis to my home. Nellis AFB is where we had been based, and we had lived in Las Vegas, which is almost due south from Nellis. But I have always considered Iowa my home, and that, of course, is almost due east of Nellis.

The next day there was 10,000 foot overcast, and the A-7s punched down through it and found me again. The leader called me and said: "Hey, did you know you were right up against a house?" Well, I didn't of course, and I moved away from it while they strafed the house and environs. The jungle instructors had told us about the water vines they picked up a lot of return fire, and told me that I was going to have to move to an area that was not quite so hot. In the meantime, they dropped a survival package that contained water, food, and batteries for my survival radio, which was getting weaker every time I used it. They gave me directions to the package and headed home.

I knew it was a hot area, because I had heard AK-47s firing at them from pretty close to my position. I had to decide whether it was best to just get the hell out of that area as quick as possible, forgetting the water in that package, or to go for that water. By this time, I was really thirsty, and the vote was 51 to 49 in favor of the water. I cautiously made for the area in which they had said the package had fallen. Suddenly, I came to a pretty well beaten path. I looked both ways and stepped gingerly across. The trip wire they had strung at the edge of the trail was practically invisible, and the explosive cap that announced it's disturbance was the first indication that I had snagged it. I dove into a thicket of brush, but they had heard the cap go off, and the area was swarming with them in no time at all. It didn't take them long to spot me. Then they just stood around jabbering and pointing at me. Finally, they got some guy to come up and tap me on the shoulder. I knew it was all over.

I stood up and made a gesture of surrender, and they were all over me. Funny thing, the first thing to come off was my Seiko watch . . . then they got around to my gun and knife. They stripped me down to my underwear and boots and marched me down the hill to a base camp they had set up as a holding area to await a truck to come out from Hanoi and get me. I had been on the ground, evading them, for a week.

F-111A with 16 CBU58s. Each CBU contains 800 1 lb. bombs. These were used for SAM site suppression, and did a great job of making the gunners keep their heads down. (Roger Peterson)

Loaded with four 2,000 lb. Mk 84 bombs, used against "hard" targets. (Roger Peterson)

Mk 82 Snakeye high drag bombs were used for low level deliveries. (Roger Peterson)

(Above & Below) Roger Peterson, about to climb aboard for a combat mission with the 429th TFS. Combat gear includes survival vest, pistol, and "G" suit. During their five month combat deployment, the 474th dropped over 74,000 bombs. F-111 combat missions were flown without the support of ECM aircraft, tankers, MIGCAP fighters, or Wild Weasel SAM suppressors, making them the most cost-effective bombers in the Vietnam War. (USAF)

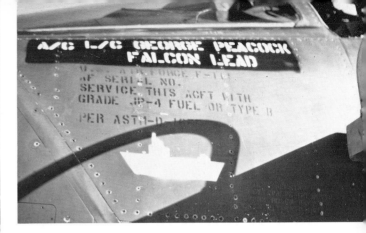

F-111s participated in the Mayaguez rescue effort, sinking Cambodian gunboats. (Don Logan)

During combat deployment, support crews from other SAC and TAC F-111 units were sent to the 474th TDY, in order to gain experience in a combat situation. (USAF)

The first of seven F-111Bs built by Grumman, on its first flight from Calverton, May 18, 1965. (Grumman)

The B model's wings were each 3½ feet longer than the A's, one of the design requirements for operating from carriers. Another was the shortened nose, a concession to the limited parking space aboard ship. (Grumman)

Nose Development

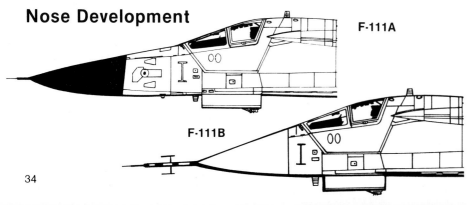

F-111A

F-111B

F-111B

Intended as the U.S. Navy replacement for the F-4 Phantom, the F-111B was the version that would have proven the commonality concept....had it worked. The Navy would have received a total of 231 F-111Bs, which theoretically would have served in the 1968 to 1975 time period.

The third F-111B was used as the test aircraft for the Hughes Phoenix Missile System. It scored a direct hit on a drone with its first firing, and by the time the F-14 came along, the AWG-9/Phoenix had been developed to a high degree of reliability. Unfortunately, the F-111B got further and further away from commonality with its Air Force counterparts, and when Congress killed it in 1968, the Navy left its 111s to waste away. (Roger Besecker via Jim Sullivan)

F-111C

Australia operates two squadrons of the F-111 (Numbers 1 and 6, based at Amberley, Queensland). The Australians were the first foreign power to enter into negotiations to acquire the TFX, completing agreements on May 28, 1966, with the signing of an order for 24 aircraft. Britain had agreed to the purchase of 50 F-111Ks at the same time, under the impression that they had found a "cheap" alternative to their TSR-2. The F-111C program was delayed by the same problems plaguing the F-111A, and in 1970 the Australian government secured the right to cancel their order without the loss of capital investment, whereupon the F-111Cs were dismantled and stored. In the meantime, the Australian government were provided F-4Es on a lease-back arrangement, pending final disposition of their F-111C order. When the F-111 structural problems had been worked out, Australia opted to go ahead with their acquisition upon completion of the necessary modifications to the wing carry-through box structure. But in the meantime, the per aircraft price had risen from less than 4 million dollars to 24 million dollars! Training of Australian aircrews was extended and fine-tuned with the intention of attaining zero attrition, with the result that Number 82 Strike Wing did not become operational until 1975.

RAAF F-111Cs are basically F-111As, with the longer wing of the FB-111A, strengthened landing gear to accomodate the heavier gross weight of the C, and bigger tires. Cockpit is the same as the F-111A, except that the righthand control stick is removable. They are illustrated here over Brisbane, which is close to their base of RAAF Amberley, and at the Kwajalein Missile Range. Camouflage is similar to USAF patterns and colors for the F-111A. (RAAF, DOD)

F-111E

The second tactical version of the F-111, the E model, became operational in October 1969, at Cannon AFB, New Mexico. The F-111E introduced the redesigned intakes, designated "Triple Plow 2". They are moved out 4 inches from the fuselage, and the center cone geometry is changed to improve engine performance at high speed, high altitude, and during high alpha flight maneuvers. Avionics of the E are similar to those of the A except for the addition of advanced TFR and a strike camera. The E also has automatic ballistics computing capability, and its combat survivability is enhanced with the addition of improved ECM. All E models are equipped with the TF-30-P3 engines.

20th TFW F-111E taxiing out to an active runway. (Michel Klaver)

F-111E of the 20th TFW, RAF Upper Heyford, England. The revised intakes are clearly visible in this view. Their introduction removed flight restrictions above mach 2.2 and 60,000 feet. (USAF)

F-111E lifts off with afterburners cooking. The TF-30 engines, which have caused many of the F-111 development problems, were also the first jet engines qualified for supersonic flight at sea level. Their afterburners, unlike conventional turbojet afterburners, are capable of zonal settings. (USAF)

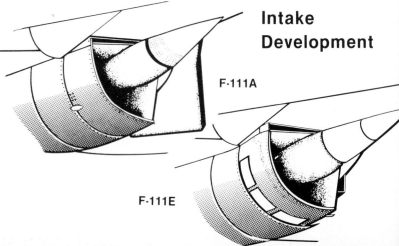

Intake Development

F-111A

F-111E

F-111E landing approach. (USAF)

20th TFW F-111E.

F-111E maintenance at RAF Upper Heyford. F-111s employ no drag chute for braking, but they do have a tailhook for use with runway arrestment gear. Large main gear uses disc brakes with anti skid system. (USAF)

F-111E of the 77th TFS, 20th TFW, June 1972. Loaded with six Mk 82 inert bombs for display purposes. Also note refuelling receptacle atop fuselage in open position. (Norman E. Taylor)

F-111D

The F-111D is the third version built for TAC. It was the first of the F-111 family to get the more advanced Mk II Avionics Package, which includes the AN/APQ-130 attack radar, AN/AYK-6 digital computer, AN/APN-189 Doppler navigation system, AN/APQ-128 TFR, and the AN/APS-109C RHAW and CADC (Radar Homing and Warning and Central Air Data Computer.) The Mk II avionics are built by North American Rockwell's Autonetics Division and feature microelectronic circuitry to improve reliability and power and to reduce weight. Continuous airborne system self-test and built-in ground test features assure accurate performance. The Mk II system provides multimode air-to-air target detection and conversion regardless of weather and clutter, improved air-to-ground weapons delivery, improved visual and radar target detection and identification as well as other advanced features. The attack radar gives the F-111D increased air-to-air capability. It can detect and track airborne targets in clutter and provides a narrow continuous beam for use by semiactive radar homing missiles. The digital computer replaces the analog computer of the F-111A and E. A horizontal situation display shows the aircraft position, bearing, ground track and destination superimposed over navigation maps or reconnaissance photos. The F-111D incorporates the intakes of the F-111E, but matches them to the improved TF-30-P9 engines.

F-111D is flown only by the 27th TFW. Rotating gloves at leading edge of wing root deflect to 40 degrees to provide additional lift during takeoff and landing, and to allow operation of slats with wings fully forward. Also obvious in this picture is the difference in deflection inboard and outboard on slats. (Dave Menard via Jerry Geer)

Flight of F-111Ds from 27th TFW, Cannon AFB, N.M. The F-111D began to come off the production line in the fall of 1970, and replaced the 27th's A models beginning in 1971. (USAF)

366th TFW, Mountain Home AFB, is one of two units flying the best of all F-111s, the F-111F. The other is the 48th TFW, RAF Lakenheath, England. (General Dynamics)

The F-111F is the last tactical 111 to be manufactured, but it is also the most expensive, 82 of the Fs costing as much as 350 111s were projected to cost at the beginning of the TFX program, in 1961. (Peter Mancus)

F-111F of the 366th TFW, at Forbes AFB in August 1974. (Jerry Geer)

F-111F

The penultimate tactical version of the F-111, the F model incorporated the best of all preceding versions and added power in the TF-30-P100 engines, which produce 25% more thrust than the early versions. The avionics package is designated Mk IIB and is simpler yet more advanced than the preceding Mk II package. And, best of all, the avionics package costs half of what the Mk II package ran. Though the F model is a growth version in every sense of the word, incorporating all the airframe and avionics changes dictated through experience with the preceding models, it would not have been built had it not been for the astounding performance increase of the P100 engine. The F-111F is the first aircraft of any kind to employ in standard construction the use of boron/epoxy laminates.

39

FB-111A

Conceived as an interim bomber to bridge the gap between the B-52-B-58 combination, and the ultimate manned bomber, the B-1, the FB-111A is basically an F-111D with the longer wings of the Navy F-111B, and the more powerful TF-30-P7 engines. Early FB-111As retained the A-style intake, but later production models had the revised E intake. The original plan was to buy 263 FBs, which would have replaced the B-58 and the B-52C, D, and F models. In 1965, it was thought that these aircraft could be bought for 1,750 million dollars. After McNamara left office, Congress cut the total buy to 76 aircraft, which ended up costing 1,200 million dollars. The FB-111 has proven itself to be an extremely effective bomber, placing first in SAC's bombing competition within two months of joining the active force. The FB-111A is capable of carrying conventional or nuclear weapons and, in tests with the SRAM (Short Range Attack Missile) in which firings were conducted down to 300 feet AGL at targets in all quadrants, the FB-111A bettered required performance by over 50%.

The last of the initial 18 pre-production F-111As was developed as the FB-111A. The first FB-111 accepted by SAC entered the inventory in October 1969. It continued a long line of Convair/General Dynamics strategic bombers, starting with the B-24 and including the B-36 and B-58. Completion of the FB-111A production run brought the total of these bombers to 3,444. (General Dynamics)

BOMBER/TANKER AIRCRAFT ACCIDENT COMPARISON
AT FIRST 100,000 FLIGHT HOURS (CUMULATIVE)

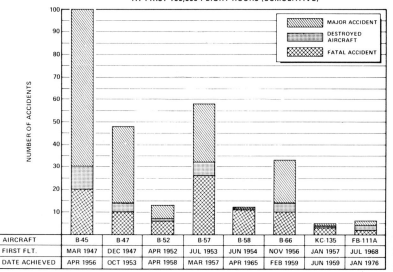

Legend:
- MAJOR ACCIDENT
- DESTROYED AIRCRAFT
- FATAL ACCIDENT

NUMBER OF ACCIDENTS

AIRCRAFT	B-45	B-47	B-52	B-57	B-58	B-66	KC-135	FB-111A
FIRST FLT.	MAR 1947	DEC 1947	APR 1952	JUL 1953	JUN 1954	NOV 1956	JAN 1957	JUL 1968
DATE ACHIEVED	APR 1956	OCT 1953	APR 1958	MAR 1957	APR 1965	FEB 1959	JUN 1959	JAN 1976

First FB-111A shown loaded with four 750 gallon auxiliary fuel tanks and dummy SRAMs on inboard pylons. FB-111s do not carry the Vulcan cannon, retaining weapons carrying capability for the weapons bay. (General Dynamics)

FB-111A

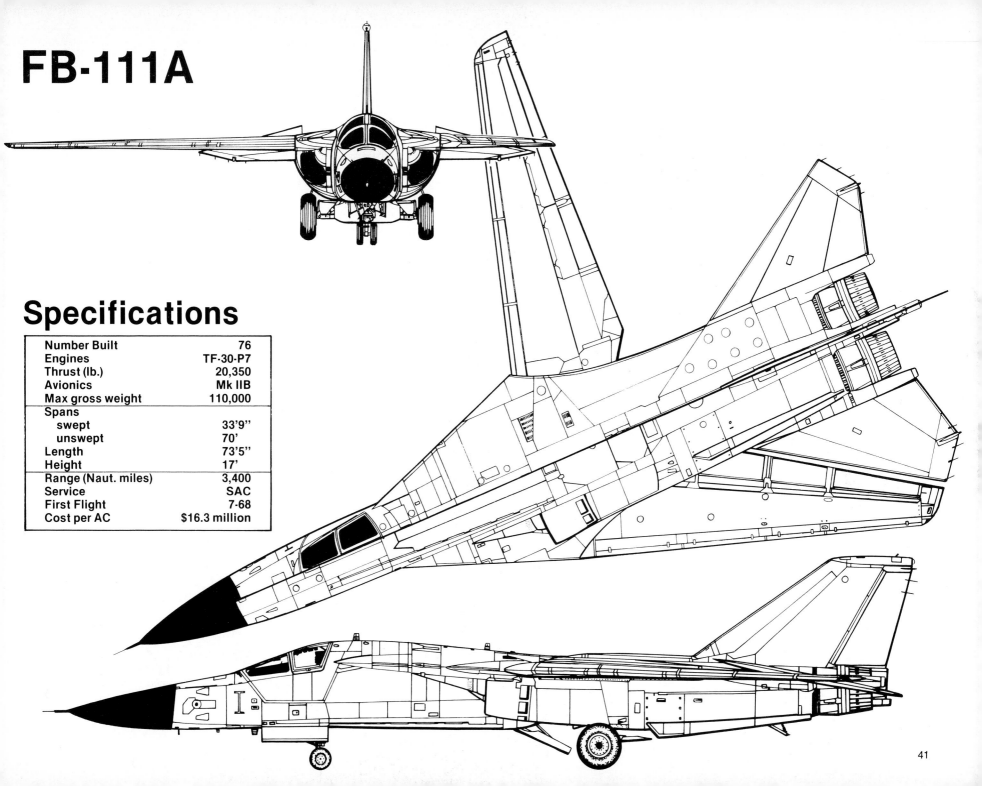

Specifications

Number Built	76
Engines	TF-30-P7
Thrust (lb.)	20,350
Avionics	Mk IIB
Max gross weight	110,000
Spans	
swept	33'9"
unswept	70'
Length	73'5"
Height	17'
Range (Naut. miles)	3,400
Service	SAC
First Flight	7-68
Cost per AC	$16.3 million

First of the second batch of five FB-111As was equipped with strike camera atop vertical fin to record test activities. Insignia appears to be Snoopy in the cockpit of FB-111A . . . but going backwards . . . ? (General Dynamics)

FB-111A during test program, with weapons bay open, prior to test firing of SRAM. Black circled white dots on fuselage are to aid in photo interpretation of aircraft maneuvering during tests. (General Dynamics)

Air scoop inboard of intake is for secondary air system, which provides environmental control system air as well as a means to vent the engine cavity. This air is vented at mid-fuselage and rear ports, preventing the formation of dead air, which in turn improves aerodynamics. (General Dynamics)

FB-111A equipped with four dummy SRAMs, also has four cameras mounted to record launch of weapons. (USAF)

FB-111A with spoilers in full up position. Relatively small size of FB-111 makes it a difficult target for enemy radar to acquire. (General Dynamics)

Fuel dumping in FB-111 is a spectacular exercise, as the jettisoned fuel is ignited by engine exhaust. (General Dynamics)

509th Bomb Wing FB-111A carried the 2nd Air Force winged deuce in 1974.

SAC FB-111s have now been equipped with updated ECM equipment in the form of the ALR-62 RHAW, which provides the crew with prioritized threat data. (Don Logan)

ECM equipment is housed in "speed bumps" on either side of exhaust nozzles. FB-111As have a wingspan seven feet greater than tactical versions of the F-111, and larger tires and brakes to accomodate the increased payload of the SAC version. (General Dynamics)

SAC operates two wings of FB-111As, the 380th at Plattsburgh AFB, N.Y. and the 509th at Pease AFB, N.H. The 509th Bomb Wing dropped the first Atomic Bomb on Japan, with the B-29 "Enola Gay".

FB-111A with four SRAMs on moveable inboard pylons. FB-111 is equipped with two
identical IBM digital computers which function
as navigation and weapons delivery computers. (USAF)

FB-111H

The career of the F-111 seems destined to forever be inextricably bound to politics, and the probably never-to-be-built "H" model is no exception.

During the early 1970s the USAF and General Dynamics embarked upon a program to modernize and extend the life of the FB-111A. For the first three years of this program the improvements were in the form of technological advances applied to the existing airframe/engine combination. In 1974 it became obvious to General Dynamics

that they could not go much further with the basic FB-111 design, whereupon they began work on a much more radically modified version of the F-111. Because of the Air Force determination to develop and buy the B-1, this program was not publicized. When Jimmy Carter decided that keeping an ill-advised campaign promise was more important than maintaining the integrity of the TRIAD strategic concept (ICBMs, missile-launching submarines, manned penetrating bombers) and cancelled the B-1, the FB-111H was catapulted into the limelight. Unfortunately, the timing of this introduction made it seem as though General Dynamics had whipped up a cheap alternative to the B-1 overnight in order to capitalize on the strong Congressional sentiment in favor of maintaining a viable manned penetrating bomber force into the next century. Nothing could have been further from the truth. When the FB-111H was introduced, General Dynamics had already expended over $10,000,000 of its own discretionary funds on development. Scale models of the FB-111H had undergone over 800 hours of wind tunnel testing.

The program presented to Congress in 1977 proposed modification of two FB-111As into FB-111Hs. After testing and approval of the design, an additional 65 FB-111As would be rebuilt to "H" configuration, followed by manufacture of 98 new FB-111Hs. The FB-111H would be a versatile aircraft, with missions of nuclear weapons delivery, conventional weapons delivery, cruise missile launch, limited response, and ocean surveillance. Estimated cost for the first 65 FB-111Hs was from 35 to 42 million dollars each. (The difference being to cover inflation.) Though not as effective as the B-1, the FB-111H would provide USAF with an excellent penetration bomber until the BX could be developed and brought into the inventory. (The BX was envisioned as the ultimate manned penetration bomber.)

If the Air Force thought half a loaf (the FB-111H) was better than none, (no B-1) the Congress had other ideas. Apparently, members of Congress felt that approving further study funding for the FB-111H would get President Carter off the hook with some of his critics within the military, who were not at all convinced that Carter's choice of the cruise missile, carried by tired B-52s or modified wide-body transports, was a viable alternative to a new manned penetration bomber. In a kind of reverse psychology, the Congress deleted study funding for the FB-111H, saying: "We are sending a message that is clear and consistent, and it will be clear to the Department of Defense that what we want them to do is to be honest and fair with the legislative body and ask for what they really want (The B-1)." As of this writing, they have gotten neither the FB-111H nor the B-1.

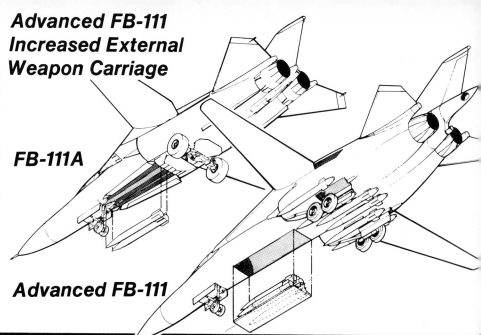

Advanced FB-111 Increased External Weapon Carriage

FB-111A

Advanced FB-111

EF-111A made its first flight on May 17, 1977, spending over two hours in the air, during which time emitters were detected, identified, located and jammer assignments effected. (Grumman)

EF-111A

The extremely high air defense threats encountered in modern warfare have made the Electronic Warfare aircraft an absolute necessity in today's Air Force, and the EF-111A will replace obsolescing EB-66s and EB-57s in the USAF inventory. The mission of the EF-111A will be to provide the tactical strike forces with high-power steerable, directional ECM jamming against early warning, height finder, ground control intercept, and acquisition radars in three basic areas of operation. In the barrier stand off mission, EF-111As will orbit near the boundary between friendly and enemy forces, jamming the early warning and other long range surveillance radars. This jamming "screen" denies the enemy information on operations in friendly airspace, be it the forming up of a strike or routine logistics operation. The essential element of surprise is maintained. The close air support mission brings the EF-111As to the forward edge of the battle area to suppress the enemy's air defense while the strike force delivers its weapons. The penetration escort mission calls upon the EF-111As to cross over into hostile air space, accompanying tactical strike aircraft to high priority targets deep behind enemy lines. The EF-111As screen the strike aircraft by continuously jamming all the electronic air defense elements along the flight path. It is in the latter mission that the EF-111As speed and range stand it in good stead, giving it a much higher survivability than its slower predecessors.

Grumman was chosen as prime contractor for the EF-111A, based upon their experience with the F-111B and the ALQ-99 jamming system, which is carried by the Grumman EA-6B Prowler. The ALQ-99E is the latest version of the proven jamming system, and has been improved and simplified for installation in the EF-111A.

The concept of marrying a proven jamming system to a high performance aircraft began evolving in the early 1970s. The Air Force selection of the F-111A was based on its availability from inventory as a sunk-cost asset, and its adaptability to the carriage and housekeeping of the required 5,000 lbs. of electronics equipment. It has demonstrated structural durability and long-loiter characteristics, and it is compatible with the other elements of the strike forces in terms of maneuverability and supersonic performance.

Active adaptation of the Jamming Subsystem to Air Force requirements and the F-111A began during the competitive design study/risk—reduction Phase IA in early 1974. Full-scale development work began with the award of a Phase IB contract to Grumman in January 1975.

The EF-111A has an operating envelope in excess of Mach 2.1 at altitudes up to 50,000 feet and is supersonic at sea level. It carries over 32,000 pounds of fuel, allowing it to stay airborne for 4½ hours unrefueled. (Grumman)

Second prototype EF-111A is finished in overall low-reflectivity gray paint. Principle external modifications include a 16 foot long pod under the fuselage, which houses transmitting antennas for ECM gear, while the pod on top of the vertical fin contains receiving antennas. (Grumman)

EF-111A will provide the jamming protection which strike forces in Southeast Asia did not have. Those strike forces were monitored by North Vietnamese long range radars from the time they took off until they returned to base. This EF is painted in a special red, white and blue scheme. (Grumman)

Tail Development

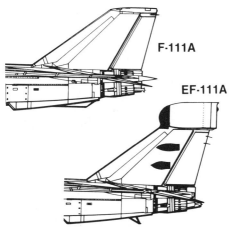

F-111A

EF-111A

A pair of F-111Fs were modified with PAVE TACK pods for flight tests at McClellan AFB, California in late 1977. PAVE TACK system contains a forward looking infrared sensor to enable aircraft crews to search for, acquire and track targets at night, and in marginal weather conditions. It will give the crews real time imagery equivalent to black and white TV pictures, and will enable them to improve accuracy of conventional weapons, or to guide "smart" bombs. (General Dynamics)

The thirteenth F-111A was modified with a supercritical wing, which is thicker, and has a longer cord with less span than the normal F-111A wing. This was accomplished in a joint USAF/NASA program, in an effort to improve high subsonic cruise performance, and to upgrade combat maneuverability. Wing sweep of the PROJECT TACT F-111A ranges from 10 degrees full forward to 58 degrees fully swept. (Don Logan)

Aircraft Armor Weapons Warship

squadron/signal publications

IN ACTION